The People's Hist

Memories Of Bedlingtonshire And Beyond

by

Evan Martin

The original seal of Bedlingtonshire Urban District Council.
Wansbeck District Council took over administration in 1974.

Previous page: Bedlingtonshire UDC wagon with Coal Queen, Jill McNair and
other village beauties at the Miners' Picnic in 1954. (Photograph Wm Ward).

Copyright © Evan Martin 2001

First published in 2001 by

The People's History Ltd
Suite 1
Byron House
Seaham Grange Business Park
Seaham
Co. Durham
SR7 0PY

ISBN 1 902527 77 1

Contents

A more recent (*circa* 1960s) photograph of one of the oldest parts of Bedlingtonshire. Sheepwash goes back a long way in Bedlingtonshire's history. Still called 'Shipwish' by many of the locals, it is a picturesque spot and is today, as in the past, visited by trippers on a fine summer's day.

Introduction

For the past 30 years I have done the rounds of women's institutes, guilds, church groups, rotary clubs and others, giving talks and slide shows. The subjects have varied from local history, mainly of Bedlingtonshire, to stories of my life as a primary school teacher. The local dialect comes into it too, as I am keen on its preservation in some form.

Having covered most of Northumberland, parts of County Durham and Newcastle with my talk trekking, it has often been suggested to me that I put the anecdotes and accounts into print.

This I've thought about, but have always been aware of the fact that telling a story orally is a lot easier to fashion than having to write it. People's reading speeds and the difficulty in reading dialect words would surely affect the sharpness of the tale. I have been assured by those who have previewed this book that the humour comes through where it has to. It is hoped you too find this so.

This book is a mixture of tales of my young life in the colliery rows and the happiness I found there; my working life thereafter and some illustrations of local and historical interest.

Almost all the tales are based on actual happenings although in some cases names have been changed and in one story a hint of the apocryphal is obvious.

Whatever your approach to reading this, the aim is for you to enjoy it, with maybe a laugh or two as a bonus.

Some friends have added contributions and everything considered, there should be something for everyone with a sense of humour and nostalgia in their make-up.

Evan Martin
September 2001

Acknowledgements

My thanks are offered to the following people who so kindly helped in the production of this book:

Nancy Appleby, Alan Buckham, Father Colin Carr, Andrew Clark, Ronnie and Doreen Cole, Ted Cremen, Colin Crosby, Margaret Crosby, Harry Dobson, Ann Donohoe, Jack Dunsmore, Marian Easton, Ethel Elliott, Yvonne Gallon, Edna Halligan, Jack Holliday, Howard Milburn, Betty and Jim Middlemass, Bob Millican, Marjorie Neave, Linda Nicholson, Pat and Jim Robinson, John Simpson, Adelaide Snowdon, Doris and Percy Snowdon, Keith Stewart, Ernie Swailes, David and Mary Tait, Mary Wade and Bill Ward.

Special thanks to my wife Judith, for the hours spent typing and proofreading.

The book is dedicated to the memory of my mother and father, Alice and Stephen Martin.

EARLY EVENTS

The author just before the wasp invasion.

It is obviously not in the memory bank, but I'm assured I was 'befriended' by a swarm of bees when eight months old. Born at Barrington Colliery in 11 Middle Row, 'Pop' Hay, the colliery pollis, was a beekeeper who lived two doors up from us. Apparently, one afternoon, mother set me out for a kip in my coach (pram). Pop's bees took a fancy and settled on the second hand 'Queen of the Road'. The screams could be heard at Bedlington Station until Pop somehow got the swarm back to its hive.

Seemingly, I was unhurt, didn't wake up and I'm here to tell the tale.

Thirty years later I applied for the job of headteacher at Acklington Primary School. My application form was received at the staff section in Northumberland Education offices and I took a call shortly after from someone in staffing: 'Do you know anything about bees Mr Martin?'

'Yes,' I replied. 'I know I hate them'.

That was enough for the scrapping of my application for that particular headship, where apparently beekeeping was as important as the teaching of Maths and English.

Barrington Colliery as it was *circa* 1870. Barrington was a typical colliery village, built around the pit shaft and then, like West Sleekburn and Netherton, virtually abandoned on closure of the pits.

Moving On

In 1938 Dad got a deputy's job across the fields at Bomarsund Colliery. A colliery house was his at the Bomar (geographically Stakeford, but the houses were inhabited by Bomarsund miners).

I became so attached to that house in West Terrace, next to Eliza and Tom Smailes, that when Dad had the chance of a bigger house in the pit yard (Office Houses) I didn't sleep for a week worrying in case we had to move (all of 200 yards). We thankfully stayed, and the Martins occupied 51 West Terrace for fifty three years.

During the war years, Dad was often on ARP duty at nights. My mother wasn't aware of air raid warnings because of her hearing loss and Mrs Lake on one side and Eliza on the other banged twice on the walls to warn us of potential bombing. This inspired us to take to the safety of the 'dark hole', a cupboard under the stairs, where Mam had a deck chair and I a makeshift bed. Three bangs meant the 'all clear' had gone and we were back to normal.

A bomb dropped in the fields behind the allotments around 1943-44. We were told it hadn't gone off, but it certainly rattled the windows and caused much diving under kitchen tables, with the impact recoil.

The war years meant total blackout in the rows. Even the 100 watt colliery street lamp was doused at Eliza's corner. My big pal at the time was Billy Wilkin. One night he'll not forget was when he was four and I was three. He lived at 49 East Terrace almost opposite our 51 West. Often Billy popped across for company and this particular winter's evening he'd played with my soldiers and fort (made by Mr Hopper at 48 West Terrace) and helped himself, as I had, to Mam's plateful of store raisins (supplied by Jimmy Hunter). Seven o'clock came and

West Terrace and East Terrace, Bomarsund. The Barrington Colliery band leads the Gala procession past The Green (now Liddell's of Stakeford).

mam opened the back door to let Billy out and across the lane. I decided the raisins had worked too well and Mam quickly provided a bucket which was thankfully used and carried over the yard to the netty, where unknown to anyone, Billy was sitting; he also having been taken short by the raisin attack.

Mother didn't see him and he was covered by the bucketful and nearly flushed away as she, in one movement, tipped the pail and pulled the chain.

Billy, according to Dad who was at the back door, moaned with an extended 'Ugh', which just about summed up his feelings.

My mother washed Billy's clothes and Mrs Wilkin saw the funny side of the situation, but I'll bet Billy Wilkin still remembers that night in the netty of nearly sixty years ago.

Continuing the theme of privvies. I remember many years later giving a talk at the British Legion ladies group at Bedlington Station. I showed a slide to the group of Tommy Coxon, the Red Row milkman, dishing out milk at what I described as Phoenix Row. This was opposite the Palace Cinema in the vicinity of what is now the health centre.

An elderly lady interrupted the discourse to ask me, 'Waat didyi say thi caaled that place, hinny?'

'Phoenix Row,' I echoed.

'Ay, aa wis born in that street, lived there 'til aa wis married and thi nivvor caaled it that. It wis alwis P... Pot Raa on accoont o' the wives weshin the chambers oot at the bottom i' the raa's tap and puttin thim t'dry o' the rain barrels.'

Tommy Coxon, before the First World War, selling milk down Phoenix Row.

'That's interesting', I said, trying to regain order through the laughter.

The lady finished what had been her little session by adding, 'Thi wa nearly elwis dry bi dinner time. The wives wud tyek thim in and put the stotty cyecks oot t' cool in tha place.'

Enjoying Ourselves

Most of our entertainment, as kids, was self-provided. Quiet games like chucks and milkies pleased us as young lads and the lasses liked skipping, two bally and bays with the hitchy dabber among others. Nothing, in any of the coalfields, took the place of the open field (in our case The Rec), and we played football until we were dog tired. So many natural sportsmen were raised in the colliery rows, it's no surprise league scouts were regular attenders at school and youth club matches. Footballers like Jimmy and Bill Thompson, Tommy Spratt, 'Pud' Barnfarther, Brian O'Neill, John Stafford and George and Alan Trewick are only a few who come to mind as playing for league clubs.

Sadly, cricket isn't played as much in local schools as it used to be. We in Bomarsund are very proud of our cricket team which, made up of local lads, won the national Haig Village trophy at Edgbaston in 1974.

Bomarsund's achievement was magnificent and highlighted the cricket which has been played in the Shire villages for over 100 years.

Barrington's last game was played at Bedlington Cricket Club and these lads in white posed on Bank Holiday Monday in 1946 for the last ever photograph of the Barrington side. Back row, left to right: Bobby Simpson, Peter Scott, Steve Tucker, Billy Poppit, Tom Brodie. Middle row: Tom Scott, Jack Scott, Tommy Dickinson, Joe Riddle, Ronnie Cole. Captain, in front: Bill Ritchie.

'The Fret' was our evening relaxation place and four changes of show per week often meant four visits to the makeshift cinema (posh name 'The Lyric') to watch the show, flick orange peel into the beam and hear manageress Bessie Richardson shout 'How, Eee, Oot!' to boisterous young clients.

The Stakeford and Bomarsund War Memorial Hall was the correct name for 'The Fret' having been erected with the Workmen's Institute next door in the early 1920s.

Occasionally dances were held, but the highlight of the year for us teenagers were the amateur dramatics productions which gave ordinary housewives and miners the chance to show how near they were to emulating Vivien Leigh and Clark Gable.

Probably the most popular amateur dramatics group in our area was the Ellesmere Players who practised and performed in the old scouts hut behind Gleghorn's Shop.

Some of the performances were very good and everyone had a line, even the hangers on. One night a group of us went to the Friday evening performance and creased ourselves at an important part of the third act. Percy Turnbull (Porcy Tornbull) had one line to say. He'd practised it for weeks and when he came on, in his excitement pronounced: 'Hark, I thurt I hord a cuckoo.'

The Ellesmere Players on stage in the early 1950s. Included are: Jimmy Monroe, Doris Wilkin, Mrs Monroe, Bill Watson and Eva McNair.

Bedlington Grammar School Drama Club, 1955. Some of the players, from the left, are: Ann Storey, Eileen Teasdale, Marian Robinson, Peter Glass, Pat Dodds, Shirley Davison, Una Warren, Bob Joisce, Valerie Foreman, Ron Henderson, Bill (Bootsie) Brown, Evan Martin, David (Flash) Harvey, John Wade.

Amateur dramatics were very popular throughout Bedlingtonshire and were well supported until recent years.

Percy's foible with his one liner shows our particular area has a lovely way of inventing words. Unfortunately the closing of the pits mainly, has taken away some of our creations. Television, radio, computers, mean people can now see and hear the English way of pronunciation. We still have people with 'arthuritis' who will wait forever in a 'cassuallity' ward for attention. I don't suppose I'll meet anything to match the man who asked me into his late father's house to value furniture.

There was a decided pong about the place, traceable through the baccy smoke.

'Aam sorry aboot the smell', volunteered the lad. 'Me faather wis intercontinental yi knaa.'

A Methodist Upbringing

Bedlingtonshire villages had strong Methodist Chapels. Most had Wesleyans at one end and Primitives at the other. In Cambois and The Winnin' they were nicknamed the Pen & Ink (Wesleyans) and the Pick & Axe (Primitives) or names of similar meaning to distinguish between the two. Often the two grades didn't see eye to eye and sometimes fell out with one another.

In the late 1940s the then vicar of Choppington decided that seeing

The original Stakeford Primitive Methodist Chapel on right.

we all worshipped the one God, Methodists and Church of England should get together and form a unified Church.

A meeting was arranged with local chapel leaders and it was decided a joint service would be held at the Stakeford Chapel. This would involve Methodists of both persuasions from Bomarsund, Stakeford and West Sleekburn (The Winnin'). The evening meeting on a Sunday night in March saw the Winnin' folk come across on the No 44 bus, the Primitives on one side and Wesleyans on the other. The service was run by the vicar of Choppington and Bob Haigh, a passionate Primitive, for the Methodists. The Church of England brought their own organist and hymn books (Ancient & Modern) and the Methodist Hymn Book was also in operation with Jack Anderson at the keyboard. We had 'Oh God our help in Ages past' from the Church of England and played with decorum by the lady organist from Choppington.

There was a lesson reading and then it was time for Bob Haigh to get on his feet and announce with the loudest voice 'From the Methodist Hymn Book, one of the greatest hymns ever written, 'Blessed Assurance, Jesus is Mine, Oh what a foretaste of Glory Divine. Heir of Salvation, Purchase of God. Born of his spirit, washed in his blood.'

Bob didn't need his hymn book. He knew it off by heart. His right arm was outstretched as he grabbed the pulpit rail and looked towards heaven for inspiration.

The singing which followed from the Andersons, Neaves, Rogers and the inspirational distinctive, articulation of the Winnin's own Geordie Gleghorn, I swear, lifted the roof. They sang the chorus 'This is my story. This is my song. Praising my Saviour, all the day long' three times. When Jack, the organist finished with his flourish and Jack

Randle's 'Halleluyah' rang out, everyone was visibly moved. It took Bob Haigh a good minute and a half to compose himself before making his way to the pulpit rail, wiping away the tears, pronouncing the immortal words, 'As lang as they live, the Church of England folk'll never sing like the Methodists.'

The Primitives and the Wesleyans sat together on the 44 bus back to The Winnin', but that was as near as we got to Church unity in Stakeford.

The Weekly Agenda

If you weren't sure what day it was, the ladies from the raas would put you right. Across Bedlingtonshire, in all my younger days, Monday was 'Weshin' day. The back kitchen was taken over by the poss tub or the hand pummeled washer with the necessary mangle or wringer. Rainy days saw the front room steaming with items round the range on the 'claes' horse. I admit to hating 'Weshin' day. There never seemed to be a comfortable spot to sit.

Monday, of course, was followed by Tuesday, which invariably was 'Ironing' day. This still meant clothes and sheets all over the house and we were always thankful, as kids, when Wednesday arrived and the range oven was put to use for the baking of buns, teacakes, fadges, loaves and cakes.

On Thursday, the rooms upstairs got a going over and Friday was 'Outside' day with the swilling of yards, cleaning of netties and donkey stoning of steps. Coffee and teabreaks were certainly not the norm in these days, but natters outdoors in finer weather were very common.

Before Friday passes by, let's mention that it was another day many of us young'uns faced with apprehension. With school finished for two days and a weekend to enjoy, many mothers took advantage of no school to dose us with Syrup of Figs. The expression 'Yiv nivvor been moved for a couple o' days. Ye need a gud physickin', was undoubtedly heard in many houses on a Friday night. The fact that Friday was known as bath, bash & physic night was not surprising. None of us had bathrooms and hot water from the set pot poured into the tin bath with a metal ewer, was the bath part. The bash was often what mother gave after a chase around the table with a spoonful of this dire tasting fluid in her hand. It always went down, followed by a Horlicks tablet and the announcement from Dad, that in his day it was castor oil on a Friday night, which apparently was worse than Syrup of Figs and was supposed to make me feel better. Granda, when he was there, proved how hard his generation was when he went one better by letting us all know his mother gave him and his brothers raw paraffin oil. This, apparently was poured into an open mouth while he pinched his nostrils. 'It wis elwis teckin at sivin o'clock and wis doon through wi by haff past ten.'

I forever thought how lucky it was Granda didn't smoke. He would probably have gone up in flames.

Not anywhere near as bad as Syrup of Figs was mother's own concoction to clean the skin and clear the passages: Salts & Lemon. Lemons were cut up and mixed with Epsom Salts; boiling water poured over, jugged, covered, left to settle and then forced down your neck any night or morning, not just Friday.

I didn't have a sister but my cousin Norah, Aunt Lil's eldest daughter, was as near as makes no difference. She was a lot older than me but she often stayed weekends and she and her friend Vida Tait called Friday night 'Amami Night'. This was apparently a shampoo which could make your hair like Rita Hayworth's and Margaret Lockwood's. I remember as an eight year old sending Norah's picture to Rita Hayworth in Hollywood, telling her that our Norah used Amami shampoo and asked if she like it too. A few weeks later I got an envelope, USA stamped and franked in Los Angeles, with a picture of Rita Hayworth and signed by her. She never mentioned whether or not she was an 'Amami' night girl too.

Summer days were often spent at the seaside. Cambois was a walk away along the colliery line. Blyth could be reached by the 41 bus every half hour and I loved Newbiggin best because of the 'willicks' that were bought on the Front Street, Fisher End.

Some of the remedies used 50 years ago.

Margaret Lockwood – one of Britain's favourite film stars of the 1930s and '40s.

None of those places on a fine summer's day I remember as clearly as one day in early September. We arrived at South Shields via the 42 bus to North Shields, the ferry across and the walk down Ocean Road. I can recall sitting on the beach and a local man telling my father something which disturbed him and meant our packing up and leaving for home. I understood years later that it was that day Neville Chamberlain had announced we were at war with Hitler's Germany.

Each week brought with it the daily newspaper, which I delivered, as did others, for Gleghorn's shop. The backyard sneck handle held mostly the *Newcastle Journal* or *Daily Herald*, but we lads looked for the *Adventure* and *Wizard* on a Tuesday and *The Hotspur* and *Rover* on a Thursday. Swapping went on and the adventures of Red Circle School, Wilson and Kid McGinty were regular topics for conversation. This was after we'd grown out of the *Beano, Dandy, Knockout* and *Film Fun.*

My father insisted I get Arthur Mee's *Children's Newspaper.* I found it hard work and would pretend I was reading it when I actually had *The Hotspur* tucked inside its outer covers.

My parents liked *Hulton's Picture Post* and swapped Aunt Lil for *The Illustrated.*

Television arrived for most of us in 1953 with the Queen's Coronation, but prior to that, having a radio was great. What would be tame to kids now, I thought was great. We looked forward to Raymond Glendenning's boxing commentaries and I wouldn't sleep the night before a Freddie Mills or Bruce Woodcock fight which was broadcast.

People watching the Coronation in the Rediffusion shop window in 1953.

Variety programmes were my dad's favourites. Variety Bandbox and ITMA I can remember, Derek Roy, Frankie Howerd and Tommy Handley were the stars who made my dad laugh whilst eating his 9 o'clock supper of fried egg and fritters.

A treat would be fish and chips from Coxon's Chip Shop. We usually had a long wait as it seemed Mr Coxon cooked one order at a time. Mrs Coxon kept us kids entertained by giving us words to spell. The winner getting a couple of chips.

During the war, paper was difficult to collect due to the war effort. Fish and chips were put straight onto the newsprint of the paper – no finery such as greaseproof pieces in those days.

At one time, Mrs Coxon was short of newspaper and said she would give a free bag of chips to anyone bringing ten sheets of paper to the shop.

Some of the streets' bright sparks had the notion of pinching newspapers from the back of the street lavatory cistern pipes. Mrs Coxon soon caught on and they were chased.

Almost all the lads in the raas had a nickname. The origin of some beats me. Why were the Mollon lads 'Schultz'? Why the Barnfathers 'Pud'? There was a suggestion Tom Ingham got his from a confusion with the Ingham surname. 'Migza' he was dubbed. 'Bovril' was the particularly well built Freddie Dunn who obviously thrived on beef tea. Some of the names were self explanatory like 'Lofty' (Lefty) Wilkinson who was particularly small. But others were well thought out, like 'Paxo' who when there was a debate around the club bar, had theories nobody else could understand. He was thought of as a bit of a wise guy, or sage so was dubbed 'Paxo' (after the sage and onion stuffing). 'Hoot' Gibson, 'Tiddles' Etheridge and 'Buttons' Marshall were other quaint namings.

There was 'Daggie' Moor, most probably named after Dagwood, the American cartoon character.

A story my dad always associated with Daggie was of a visit to London to see 'The Toon' play Arsenal in the 1951 FA Cup Final. A busload went from Bomarsund and when they got to the outskirt of the capital, stopped at an ABC café for refreshments. Imagine the baffled look of the counter assistant when Daggie's mate asked for a coffee and when asked what he wanted Daggie replied 'Aal hev a coffee tee'.

OUT INTO THE
BIG WIDE WORLD

The author, nineteen years of age, half way through National Service at RAF Borgentriech, West Germany.

Fellow serviceman, Guy the Golfer, at RAF Horsham St Faith, Norfolk.

Why Should England Tremble?

National Service was a two-year chore, which had to be done by lads of my age in 1956. I had seen films of forces life and most of them proved to be comedies, so I set off in September of that year ready for two years of fun. What a surprise I got. Basic training for nearly two months at RAF Hednesford in the Midlands was the worst experience of my life thus far. How any human being (our corporal) could be so horrible to others (me and fellow conscripts) I'll never know.

I saw more in those weeks than I'd seen in my previous nineteen years of school, chapel and St James' Park. We were warned against going out with women, and shown films of the possible results of affairs with the female sex that had big lads fainting about us. We were expected to be great at everything and firmly castigated if we weren't. One thing we had out of all this, without question, was discipline, and when we had our passing out parade at the end of it all, 300 of us were like a machine, marching and doing tricks with an empty rifle no-one would have believed possible at the beginning. We all had stories to tell which must have happened to every intake. We all had to 'bull' our buttons and boots and the marble effect on the toe caps of new boots was removed with boot polish, cloth and candle. One of our hut members went too far and at 2 o'clock in the morning, woke everyone up when a metal toecap he was 'de-marbling' overheated and blew up in his face. He was covered in boot polish and highly shocked; no more so than when he found out he would have to buy a new pair of boots from the stores at 16 shillings a pair. That sounds a modest amount nowadays, but in 1956 it was a hefty wack out of his 24 shillings a week pay.

We were inspected every day, bed packs, boots and drinking mugs had to be immaculate. The corporal would increase our desire to burst out laughing by picking up someone's mug with two fingers and dinky finger sticking out, asking if the owner knew there were animals inhabiting the bottom, then carefully dropping it out of the window. Anyone who did laugh, was immediately on jankers (three days cleaning toilets and washing dishes).

A haircut was essential every ten days or so. We were virtually skinheads anyway, but the typically RAF question was asked on parade, when the sergeant or corporal stood behind you: 'Am I hurting you airman?'

'No sergeant.'

'I ruddy well should be; I'm standing on your hair. Barber! Now! On the double!'

We survived the square-bashing to be posted to trade training and then to our permanent posting. There things were a little easier.

I spent 14 months at a remote radar station 8 miles from the Russian border in West Germany. We were near a US Air Force base and found they had an easier time than we had. We all wanted to model ourselves on their smart uniforms and would start by pulling the sides of our dress caps down so they looked American. Starch, hot water, some glue and clips were used to give the cap an American look. This operation unfortunately weakened the cap and it was just as well we only wore them for 'best' dress occasions, like Empire Day and Queen's birthday parades.

One parade was unforgettable when we were 'inspected' by a visiting group captain who was shown up and down the ranks only to stop in front of Taffy Hughes, a wayward Welshman from Pontypridd. His cap had been given the treatment and the senior officer pulled his peak, expecting the cap to move forward. Instead the peak came over Taffy's eyes, the ends still attached to the cap's main body. The scene was one of pure hilarity with Taffy talking to the group captain, his eyes peering between the main part of the cap and the plastic peak, which was resting on the bridge of his nose.

I spent most of my national service with Guy Henderson, a Blyth lad, who found playing sport at a high level did wonders for any serviceman. When the officers in Germany found Guy with a set of golf clubs, they were ready to ridicule him. They soon changed their tune when they found Guy was an English Youth international who played off two.

We were both eventually posted for a six-month stay in Norwich, then finished off our two-year stint twenty miles north of Aberdeen.

I couldn't wait to get home again, but in retrospect I needed that time away from home and was character strengthened by the experience.

Dad's Army of Bedlington Home Guard in the early 1940s

Working For A Living

I had the choice in my first year teaching of working at Haltwhistle or Bedlington. Naturally being of a Bedlington family, I chose the latter and found myself at the West End Junior School (The Council School) under headmaster Henry Graham. Henry allotted me a class of mixed ability 8-10 year olds, forty, when they were all there, whose faces and names I still remember to this day.

Like all primary school teachers, I covered every subject in the curriculum and tried to do it as taught at college. It took me some time to realise that good teaching performance has a lot to do with confidence and the relationship with the class which comes with experience.

I expected every child to become better each day and when I realised this wasn't happening, was very crestfallen. I would finish at four o'clock, half prepare my lessons for the following day, catch the 10A back to Stakeford and fall asleep in an armchair.

Many of the class members I still see in Bedlington and they pass the time of day, which is one of the benefits of having been in the job.

I had some laughs too. One lad who had a reading difficulty (I'll dub him 'Franky') would come out to me every morning for his reading lesson. He was ten years old and had been on pages 1 and 2 of the 'Tip & Mitten' book for 5 years. He knew those pages off by heart and would recite 'Come here Tip, come here Mitten.'

Imagine my surprise when one Monday morning he came to me with his Mawson, Swan & Morgan vocabulary book for a 'hard word' to be written for him.

Mondays, we all had stories to write about what happened in Bedlington over the previous weekend. The pieces were put on the wall to form a class newspaper 'The Bedlington Bugle'. The vocabulary books I would use to write words which pupils may find difficult.

Franky's 'hard word' turned out to be 'intend', which was very difficult for him. Nevertheless, he had asked for it, so he got it printed in his book.

The newspaper exercise took around 30 minutes, after which I collected copies in for marking during lunchtime. When I came to Franky's I couldn't decipher a word except the word I'd given him. Henry, the boss, had the answers and howled with mirth when he read out Franky's 'translated' piece. It went like this:

'On Saturday morning I played football in the back garden and kicked the ball through my dad's greenhouse window. He smacked my 'intend'.'

'Give him a mark,' said Henry, 'for using 'intend'. I can think of a lot worse words he could have used.'

Franky was a lovely lad. He is now 50, sends me a Christmas card every year, drives a 7 series BMW and is a foreman welder for BP Shell up in Aberdeen. Good for him!

My very first day in front of that class had me with Fractions to

Staff at Bedlington County Junior School, 1961. Back row: Vera Pearcey, Verna French, Nancy Hogg, Margaret Davidson, Myra Davison. Front row: John Wharrier, Henry Graham, Evan Martin.

teach. The kids knew I was green and nervous (they could probably see my knees knocking). 'Can we not have Games Sa (Sir)?'

'No its Maths,' I insisted. What's Maths? Was the general inquiry, to which I replied 'Sums.'

'We hate sums,' Tommy Dodds announced. 'What kind of sums?'

'Fractions.' I asserted.

'Nivvor heard of them sa.'

'Another name for them is portions.' I was determined to win through. 'Does anybody know what portions are?'

'Yis,' replied Tommy, 'Tha cats.'

The belt was available for use in those days, but I had to realise that Tommy was serious with his answer and nobody laughed but me. They all thought Tommy Dodds was spot on.

My first visit from an inspector was late in the school year. It was a scorching hot July day. My charges were due to leave for Westridge Secondary School and Miss White of 30 years County Hall standing, decided to visit at 2pm on the second last Friday of term.

It was important for me to pass this inspection as I was in my probationary year on £42 a month and if I 'passed' would increase my salary to £48 per month.

Art was on the timetable and everybody was so shattered with the heat I had decided to give the class a free choice.

When Miss White arrived Henry came down, told me that a freedom of choice was out of the question and as she was well into religious educational ideas, she would appreciate a Biblical theme.

We had been dealing with the Exodus, Moses leading the Hebrews out of Egypt for pastures new. 'Get them to crayon that, announced Henry. She'll love it.'

The sugar paper was duly quartered, the 'Gold Flake' tins with crayons enclosed, handed out and off they went.

Miss White appeared, well coffeed, and delighted that a Biblical theme was in motion. She accepted my Religious Education notes that morning as adequate preparation and proceeded to stealthily move up the aisle to witness the various expressions of Moses and his tribe crossing the Red Sea.

All was well until Sheila Harper's desk was arrived at. Miss White gasped and enquired as to what Sheila was drawing. 'The Crossing of the Red Sea,' I confidently offered, although I was a good yard and a half away.

'No-one with the most vivid imagination could see this as part of the Exodus,' Miss White exclaimed.

When I saw Sheila's effort, I could understand Miss White's disappointment. Moses was there, the Hebrews were there and the Red Sea was properly parted in the middle.

Unfortunately for Sheila, me, and Miss White, Moses was driving a double decker United bus through the middle with the Hebrews hanging out the windows waving their goodbyes.

Sheila had been on the Sunday School trip to Crimdon Dene the previous weekend, in a bus, driven by the Chapel Minister. Its religious similarities with her Religious Instruction lessons at school produced the piece that afternoon.

Miss White saw the funny side, said I was no longer a probationer and I could enjoy my Summer holiday knowing I would be on £48 a month from September.

It's Lovely The Way We Talk

Much has been written and preached about our local accent, the Pitmatic, Northumbrian, Geordie. To an outsider they probably all sound the same but if you've lived in the area long enough you'll know there are inflections in our speech that can distinguish the way folks talk in Stakeford and Bedlington. Certainly Blyth is obviously different, probably because of the port influence and Netherton worthies have a distinctive speech delivery.

Everyone living in our area has surely at some time met visitors especially from the South and Midlands who are befuddled by our diction.

In East Northumberland in particular the flat 'O' sound as in Bob becomes 'er' (Berb) and a herb in most other parts of the land is a seed bearing plant used for food flavouring. In our part of the world it's the top of a cooker.

A young married woman teacher, Mary Henderson, encountered a problem with this particular voice modulation when she arrived in Bedlington to teach, after living all her life in Richmond, Surrey. After a day at her primary school, she came home to inform her husband that there was a teacher with the strangest name. Her husband didn't believe her when she insisted that pupils had asked the man 'Please can we go outside and play now Mr Turd?'

Mr Todd of course was so used to this pronunciation that he thought nothing of it but it definitely sounded weird to a couple from the South.

The children in Reception at the school couldn't understand a word Mary was uttering and she had less knowledge than they did of their pronouncements. One day, about seven weeks into her time with us, Mary informed the Head she had five minutes to spare, she reckoned, at the end of her story that afternoon. Could the Head suggest something for her to do? 'Yes' said Henry. 'They're new to school and won't know about the British Legion selling poppies next Friday. Tell them about it. I'll come in and sit at the back to see how you're doing.'

Mary got through her story with few problems and the 30 odd 4 to 5 year olds had managed to cope with her strange tongue. Then she came to the British Legion part. She mentioned the fields of blood, Lord Haig and the trenches. This went down like a bomb with the little ones sitting in a semi-circle near her chair.

Then came the nitty gritty. Mary announced to them all that '... and next week the man will come from the British Legion with a big box of poppies. If you bring 5p you'll get a small poppy. 10p will get you a medium size poppy. But if you bring 50p or more ... ' Mary's patter was halted midstream by little Frankie at the front who shouted 'You'll get a greet big dog.'

A few years later, Mary Henderson was taking a class of 8 year olds and talking of groups of people, animals and things generally. She would start the grouping by announcing, 'A flock ... ?'

She then pointed to one of the risen hands and got 'Sheep.'

Proceeding with 'A gaggle of ... ?'

'Geese.' would come the answer.

This progressed wonderfully and right answers came out prolifically until she said 'A shoal of ... ?' Pointing to a lad who rarely offered an answer, he responded with 'Coals.'

Such are the vagaries of enunciation!

A lovely story heard this summer concerned a well spoken lady driving her car not far from here. She couldn't find her destination, stopped at the kerbside and asked a local lad where Tesco was.

The reply of 'The Australians are 170 for 1' left her more confused than ever and it is said she settled for Safeway shopping instead.

A Private Day In York

Having studied at St John's College, York, I knew the city fairly well and its historic value meant trips to the place were an obvious choice.

We followed a routine every time we went – a walls walk, visits to the Railway and Castle Museums and of course an amble around the Minster (which the children put another vowel in and called it the MINISTER).

A number of years ago, fire damaged parts of the Minster and the Cathedral was closed for a while. When it reopened, the crypt was made 'out of bounds' to school parties.

This was a disappointment as we'd done particular work in Bedlington on catacombs and vaults and I was looking forward to see the wonderment on the children's faces when they saw what I'd described as the 'secret and reserved' place in the Minster basement. I had the idea of contacting my old college principal, Canon Lamb, to ask if he would use his influence to get us into the crypt. He was more than willing to oblige and we were told to report to the Minster reception at a certain time and would be allowed into the crypt provided the class weren't eating crisps or swilling 'pop'. The visit was a complete success and made the children's day. The trip had been near the end of the Summer term and was just before Parents' Day. I'd had the children write of their outing and displayed their work on the classroom walls.

Parents came on their day and had a chat with me and generally said how much their boy or girl had enjoyed the York outing. One dad had a particularly big smile on his face and on enquiring as to the reason for his mirth, he asked me what we really had been doing at York. 'Have a look at what our daughter Christine's written about the visit,' he suggested.

There, displayed on the classroom wall, in a central position, with other written work was Christine's piece. She'd described the walls walk, the picnic in the gardens and finished off by telling everyone: 'Because Mr Martin knew someone in York, we were allowed to look around the private parts of the minister.'

The Incomparable Nancy

Fred Carruthers, a meticulous man, was my boss at Stobhill Junior School, where I had a post of responsibility which earned me £120 a year extra.

Student teachers at the school got a good grounding as Fred let them away with nothing. We had one particular young girl from Ponteland Training College who got into the black books in her first of six weeks with us. She (Nancy) didn't turn up to school until 11.45 on the first Friday. Her excuse was she thought it was Saturday. The reason for such an extraordinary judgement was original if nothing else. Isabel said the postman knocked on the door, which he only did on a

Saturday knowing she was out early on weekdays.

She took her parcel and was in such a stupor she went back to bed to sleep until 10.30. Coming downstairs she switched on the television to realise it wasn't 'Tizwaz' or the like, but some weekday programme.

Realising her error, she hurriedly readied herself and set forth for Stobhill. Fred was not amused, but we all laughed when she opened her parcel in the staffroom at lunchtime. It turned out to be a one armed cardigan; a Christmas present from her Auntie Mabel.

Someone pointed out she had two arms. Auntie Mabel however put our minds at rest with a note which stated: 'Sorry Nancy, I didn't have time to knit on the other arm. However the wool is from Paton and Baldwins and no doubt you'll find time to buy yourself a ball and finish the job off.'

The school at Stobhill was (and is) a double decker type with the cloakrooms jutting out the bottom section to run along and below the upstairs classrooms. Often, balls, hats, bags, etc. would be hurled up onto the cloakroom roof and I, with a special responsibility post, had to climb up the caretaker's ladder, onto the roof to retrieve the slung item. Now, I hate heights and whenever I climbed the fourteen feet up the ladder, I crawled on hands and knees to the upstairs classroom window for something to hang onto.

One particular day, I was sent to recover a small satchel, reached an upstairs classroom window, nodded to the kids, who waved to me, but I was not ready for the window opening and Nancy asking 'Did you want something Mr Martin?'

As if I would climb fourteen feet up a ladder and crawl along a ridge to ask her something!

Nancy was a star. She left us with many memories and ended up a headteacher in her native West Yorkshire, where she is still highly regarded.

My First Headship

Apply for every headship, even if you don't fancy it, was the advice of Inspector Isobel Iceton. I certainly didn't fancy Falstone, buried deep in the heart of the North Tyne Valley. My wife, Judith, would certainly say no.

The December interview day came, and the toiling journey over the Wannies through the ice and snow didn't get us off to any kind of start.

The school house was 'grotty' – large, cold, bare and isolated, well outside the village with, admittedly, a breathtaking view over the North Tyne.

Surprisingly, Judith took an immediate liking to Falstone, which helped me give an affirmative, when asked if I would like the job.

This was to be the start of a three and a half year adventure in which each day seemed to fashion something to learn from and conserve. I quickly found that my position of headmaster carried with it authority,

The beautiful village of Falstone in the North Tyne Valley.

not only within the school but throughout the immediate area.

I was only the sixth headteacher in 107 years, four of my predecessors having served long terms.

The rector and I were the only 'Misters' in the village, together with the Toms, Charlies and Harrys, and were looked upon to help with the Hunt Ball, whist drives, dances and fetes.

Judith, too, soon gained from this class elevation. She appeared in John Conkleton's shop, bought a few groceries and asked if she could have a ham shank for soup stock.

'Wi hev nen,' John rasped through his lips and a Woodbine. 'We are ee anyway?'

'We've just moved to Oakwood House,' smiled Judith.

'That's the school hoos,' John observed. 'Waat are yi deein' there?'

'I'm Judith Martin, the new schoolmaster's wife.'

John disappeared into the back shop and reappeared in no time with the meatiest ham shank we'd ever seen.

Over our years there we were to consume trout, gaffed and lawfully fished, the sweetest plums in Christendom, venison, snipe, pheasant, rabbit and turkey, all given and devoured with lashings of vegetables, carrier bagged and left on our doorstep.

The Gospel According To Stanley

Mrs Wood was nobody's fool. A first-class teacher, inspector and adviser, her word could carry enough weight at County Hall to help me find promotion. An awful lot depended on the success of her visit.

'Coffee? No I've come to see the children's work.'

Molly Wood, immaculate in Fenwick's French, was not to be sidetracked.

Audrey Kitchen, my assistant, had four new starters in the infant department, and they had settled in quite well. Mrs Wood's first love was the younger set and she could hardly conceal her delight on entering the sand slinging, paint-slapping classroom.

'Can I have a word with one or two of them?' Molly asked as she proceeded to seek out 'horrors' who had tongues halfway up their nostrils, while undertaking educational play.

One of these, in the sand tray, was a farmer's son, Stanley, who hadn't opened his mouth in the three weeks he'd been educated. His mother warned me his language was akin to the Anglo-Saxon, he having been nurtured in the fields with his father's farmhands. I assured her we were used to anything and would cope.

Mrs Wood enquired of Stanley as to his education that morning.

'Aa've dun some sums,' the lad volunteered.

'Good,' smiled Mrs Wood. 'What else have you done?'

'Scripture,' came the reply.

'Oh, I like Scripture,' said Mrs Wood. 'Who have you been learning about?'

'Some buggar caaled John the Bastard.'

Stanley had shown his colours. Amazingly, Mrs Wood survived the encounter – and so did I.

Promotion and more adventures came within the year.

The Last Farewell

Being headmaster of a small country school, certain extra curricular activities I accepted – part-time Sunday School teacher, bingo caller, Burn's Club president, Show committee member, and others. But footballer? Definitely not.

I'd played local minor football for years, but decided to retire gracefully on my appointment to Falstone School, with its necessary move into rural Northumberland. Someone, at some time, I suspect my doting father, had mentioned in the village, that I'd played regularly with Bobby Charlton. I did, for four years at Grammar School, and had been scheming inside forward with Stakeford Artisans (Second Division, Morpeth Sunday League). The expected knock on the door wasn't long in coming. Ernie Swailes, the Sir John Hall of Falstone United invited me to ' ... have a go at Jedburgh on Saturday. Wi' your job you're expected t' tek part in aal village activities.'

Now, I'd seen Falstone United in action. The eleven, mostly farmers and forestry workers, were built like brick outhouses and I couldn't see how my silky midfield skills would successfully fit into the team plan of welly, run like Hell and generally put the fear of extinction into the opposition.

This was the time when Bill Shankly was building his first fine Liverpool side. He professed that all great sides should have a classy backbone and showed his meaning by parading Scottish internationalists, St John, Yeats and Lawrence at nine, five and in goal. Ernie Swailes had the same idea and played Mattie Mather, Geordie Bell and Willie Broon in those key positions.

Mattie Mather, centre half and captain, had been known to bodily lift on stallions at the sireings. Geordie Bell, centre forward, was well known as a record pan filler at the Plashets drift mine, but Alfredo di Stefano he wasn't. Goalie, Willie Broon, had played for Falstone since before the days of Hitler, was now in his late forties, rotund, with cheeks like overripe loganberries and trained on Guinness. Willie always wore a tweed pork pie hat, before, during and after games and no matter what the goalmouth activity, that hat, like Randolph Scott's, never was seen to come off.

I capitulated, played at Jedburgh, scored in a 3-1 win and was duly selected to play in the North Tyne League Cup Final against local rivals, Wark. In the run up to the big day, talk in the village was about little else. Norman Fox's bus was booked solid, as were Billy Telfer's two cattle wagons. Bellingham showfield was the venue and the pubs in that lovely village overflowed.

Wark had a good side; league champions; they were a confident looking bunch. The crowd, of shared partiality, must have numbered a thousand and we (Falstone United) did well for an hour or so holding our opponents to a goal-less draw. Then Wark scored. Willie was beaten by a lob which saw him do a backward run, reminiscent of Fred Flintstone, before he cowped his creels on the penalty spot (his hat still attached), the ball bobbling into the net.

Falstone's heads dropped somewhat and Wark became increasingly confident, until near the end, their over exuberant centre forward charged Willie when our man had possession. Willie never budged, but cuddling the ball under his left oxter, he shot out a straight right which poleaxed Wark's number nine. Never have I seen such a melée. Standing on the opposition's eighteen-yard line, I witnessed the disappearance, into the throng, of the referee, Norman Wilkinson from Matfen, only for him to emerge seconds later with a displaced nose and his whistle back to front.

'Ivvrybody off!' yelled the official. 'Match abandoned. Yi'll aal be reported t' th' Futbal Association.'

This last pronouncement, I couldn't accept. Approaching the referee with trepidation, I politely enquired if that included me, as I hadn't done anything wrong. Lisping back, as his dentures were somewhere between the penalty spot and the centre circle, the unfortunate man spat out, 'Ee an aal, fo' argeein.'

A painting by Brian Long, originally of Cambois, of Falstone's centre. The Black Cock is the heart of the village.

All was made up, then forgotten afterwards in The Black Bull, and we tread our weary way, late on, back up the Valley.

But that wasn't the end of it for me. The following Friday out came the weekly local paper. The back page report on the game was headlined: 'FALSTONE HEADMASTER SENT OFF IN BRAWL'. I couldn't believe it. That day at 1.30pm, the phone rang in my office. The scenty Jesmond voice informed me it was the Director of Education's secretary and Mr Mellowes wanted a few words about a newspaper report.

How Charles Mellowes must have enjoyed screwing me down with his pointed questions before he lost control and his laughter signalled the end of the inquisition and the putting down of telephones. His last words to me were, 'Take my advice young man and retire gracefully.'

I never played again and ceremoniously hung up my boots in Bob Young's barn, where an owl used the laces to furnish its nest.

On leaving Falstone in 1970, I was, for a while, in headteacher limbo, waiting a few weeks until my next school was ready for me. I received a call at home one morning from Mr S.M. Smith, the man from the office in charge of Staffing. 'Do you know where Stakeford is? We'd like you to take over for a couple of days whilst the headteacher is on a course.'

Did I know where Stakeford was? Would I like a couple of days at the school? I couldn't wait to get over there and relive the happy days of my primary school life.

An Infant class at Stakeford Primary School in 1936. Back row: Alex English, Derek Middleton, Jim Charlton, Tommy Million, Peter Yeowart, Gordon Joice, Terence Buglass. Second row: Jean Gordon, Doreen Hallam, Jean Storey, Jean Ord, Enid Bryson, Joyce Richards, Mildren Grifith, Teddy Hayton. Third row: June Foreshaw, Una Godsmark, Joan Miller, Hazel Mounsey, Rita Wilkin, Esme Dunn, Lexa Deans, Winnie Deans. Front row: Harry Gilbertson, Tommy Dunn, Joe Robson, Ken Clark, Bruce Wilkinson, Jack Mounsey and Eddie Richardson.

Over The Top

My early education was set out and rounded entirely by women. Miss Newton, Miss Morgan, Miss Hay, Miss Taylor, Mrs Seeley, Miss Molden, Mrs Green and the headmistress, the redoubtable Miss Jean Smith. Miss Smith had a belt and she used it when needed. I had it once (two slaps to the right hand for climbing on the Infants yard fence). I was in good company – Jackie 'Spanner' Blaney, Eddie 'Shultz' Mollon and Tom 'Young Pud' Barnfarther were in line with me. But this lawlessness and punishment was nothing compared to the transgressions of Micky Clifton on 2nd June 1943.

The toilets in most schools were built outside the main building and Stakeford's boys' urinals were separated from the girls by a seven-foot wall. It had been the ambition of generations of Stakeford and Bomarsund lads to perform onto and over the wall so to soak the lasses on the other side. No one in 30 years had managed it, but the said Micky had a mark scratched at 6'9'' being the highest anyone had reached, until that magic morning of 2nd June 1943 when Micky went over the top, much to the chagrin of girls on the other side. They reported the happening to Miss Smith who immediately visited the boys' loo, to find daft Micky standing on George Hope's shoulders finishing off his achievement with an upward pointing arrow, his initials and the date, scratched with his pocket knife. Miss Smith lugged (literally) Micky to her office where he was given four slaps of the belt and made to stand outside her door for the rest of the day.

Twenty-seven years later, I knew that offence would have been logged. I couldn't wait to check if Micky's initials and the arrow had worn off the toilet wall; they had, but Miss Smith's Punishment Book bore the momentous entry in her fine copperplate hand. 'Pupil's name: Michael Clifton. Punishment: 2 strokes of leather belt to each hand. Reason for Punishment: Urinating to competitive altitudes.'

Micky's record was never equalled and never will be. The outside netties were thankfully pulled down many years ago.

Please Leave Me Alone

Three years at Holystone on the Coast Road, were happy times and the children, mostly from West Allotment, were biddable and a pleasure to teach.

The parents were helpful and understanding in their approach to the school. Two events involving parents are worth recounting.

At the beginning of my first term there in September 1970, I thought I'd got all the new children in when at around 10.30am (morning break time) a mother appeared at the office door with a boy (new arrival) in one hand and a little one (about two) in a pram which she left at the open office door. This pram bound youngster, the mother informed me, was 'Wor Jimmy. He's me last 'cos Aav been circumcised ye knaa.'

This statement was accompanied by Les Dawson-like facial expressions and pointings. The main object of the lady's visit was to sign 'Wor Frankie,' the second youngest, into school. While the necessary forms and questions were being dealt with, I noticed one of the teachers talking to 'Wor Jimmy' at the door. To appreciate the full colour of this story, it should be mentioned that Jimmy was sitting in his pram, hands inside the sheet, black and white woolly hat finished with bobble, pulled over his eyes, and to complete the scene he was at peace with the world, sucking on a small bottle of orange juice, which he had, in some way, rested on his jaw. It had the appearance of a netabulb and Jimmy somehow managed to breathe through his nostrils and suck through his mouth at the same time. The juice was never seen to drop. One thing was certain, he wasn't interested in teacher, Mrs Brown's, advances.

Suddenly, Mrs Brown burst out laughing, covered her mouth to stifle the mirth, went into the staffroom where there was uproar as she recounted her tale.

I couldn't wait to show Frankie and Jimmy's mother to the schoolyard, then hurried back to the staffroom to get Mrs Brown's story first hand.

The staff were still wiping their eyes when I got there. Through her tears, Mrs Brown informed me she had tried to engage wee Jimmy in conversation. He'd put up with her 'Coochy, Coochies' for about a minute and a half; then he took out his dummy and told Mrs Brown to 'Bugger Off!'

No wonder the staffroom erupted.

Mrs Gorman's Class at Barrington Village Primary School, *circa* 1959. Back row: Stephen Bushby, Derek Williamson, Brian Woolett, Alan Cowell, Henry Hall, Leslie Tiffin, Ian Bryson, Geoffrey Douglas and Ian Collis. Middle row: Margaret ?, Glenda Main, Sandra Welsh, Lynne Turnbull, Ian Carnaby, Harry Dixon, unknown, Lorraine Cuthbertson, Yvonne Black and Sandra Taylor. Front row: Jennifer Dobson, Clara Lee, Norma Dickinson, Marlene Leightley, Mrs Doreen Gorman, Susan ?, Joan White, Elizabeth Butcher and Grace ?

FAMILY TIES

The Martins. Ex-Durham Light Infantryman, Granda Stephen, wife Isabella with sons Stephen (right) and Bill (left). Taken outside 11 Middle Row, Barrington in 1926.

Some of the Neaves. Grandma Sally, Aunt Mary Ann, Aunt Lil and cousin Norah Surtees at Newbiggin in 1934.

Stephen Martin

My dad was coal mining mad. Apart from working down the pit for nearly fifty years, he spent his years of retirement delving into the history of the coalmines and villages of the area. He was very good at it too.

As a gaffer down the pit, anyone will tell you he was a non swearer. 'Flamer' was his worst expression and he was generally level headed. The only time he lost his cool was at St James' Park (a Toon fanatic) and when he was driving (he passed his test at 57 years of age.)

I remember one Saturday (October 1962) at Gallowgate we went to see United play Sunderland. The crowd was flowing up and down and we were at the Leazes End. Two huge lads were a yard or so in front of us and as the crowd surged forward a young willowy lad of 17 or 18 put his hands on their backs to stop himself falling. They both turned around and threatened the lad, if he didn't stop pushing. At this point my father called them a couple of 'Flamers' and warned them his son (all of 11 stone and decked in college scarf) would sort them out. I've rarely been as petrified in my life. Fortunately at that point the Toon scored and the crowd heaved all over the place. I'm pleased to say the two big Geordies were never see again.

As Dad got older and into his mid seventies and eighties, he realised he could speak his mind and say practically anything he liked without

A side Stephen supported as a young man, Newcastle United, 1931-32.

threat of retaliation. Some would think he's too old to thump and others took the view – He's an old man. What the heck.

To celebrate our 25th Wedding Anniversary my wife and I booked the main room at East Hartford's Lord Clyde and invited all our friends and neighbours to the 'do'. Dad was there and after the meal, whilst most danced to the disco, he was in his element sitting and talking mostly about the old days.

Peter Johnson, a good friend of mine, said he'd heard a lot about the old man and would like to meet him. 'No problem,' said I. 'Come this way.'

'Dad, this is a friend of mine you haven't met. Peter Johnson, originally from Bedlington Station,' was my opening delivery.

'Pleased to meet you. I've heard a lot about you,' said Peter.

As the hands were shaken, Dad inquired, 'Johnson, Johnson. Are you from Sleekburn?'

'Aye.' Responded Peter. 'Bank Top originally.'

'You're not 'Snuffy' Johnson's son are yi'?'

'That's right,' smiled Peter, who was chuffed there was some compatibility.

'Never liked him.' said Dad. 'And I wasn't fond of his father either.' At which point Stephen turned away, Peter howled with laughter and he bought me a drink.

I was a member of the Literary and Philosophical (Lit and Phil) Society in Newcastle a number of years ago and took my father as my guest to a lecture, by a professor of Modern History, on the Northern Coalfield and its social history. The hall was packed for the talk, complete with slides, and the evening was both successful for the speaker and interesting for the audience. Everything was going along smoothly until the chairman offered the assembly questions for the professor.

A couple of issues were dealt with successfully, until Dad put his hand up. The chairman noticed him, pointed and said, 'Yes Sir, I'm sorry I don't know your name, but you have a point to make?'

At that the old man stood up, opened up and had the gathering looking up as he announced: 'I'm Stephen Martin of Bomarsund Colliery, Bedlington. I've listened to this and enjoyed most of it, but some of it is rubbish and just not correct.' He went on to pick out and verbally correct the 'rubbish' amidst looks of astonishment. Twenty minutes later, he was given his own round of applause and had his hand shaken by the guest speaker, who became a friend for the rest of his life.

The following year, Dad took his own slides and spoke to the Lit, and Phil, thus establishing himself with the local history bigwigs, who thought he was fantastic.

Wilf Holliday

I'll always think of my dad as a wonderful father who managed to become a local councillor and gave of his time to the public as well.

Wilf Holliday was well known in Bedlingtonshire. He'd come to Bedlington Station as a young lad in 1914. He was the oldest of five brothers and one sister.

His time in local politics began in 1947 when he became the first full time secretary/agent for the Blyth constituency and Alf Robens MP until he retired in 1965.

Dad's work in the local council saw him leader until his death in 1966. He always reckoned his proudest moment was at the Miners' Picnic of 1965 when he welcomed his youngest brother Tom, who was president of the Northumberland NUM at the time. This made history as an occurrence like that had never happened before.

Jack Holliday
Bedlington, 2001

The two Holliday brothers at the 1965 Miners' Picnic. Wilf is wearing the chain of office.

John Tait The Ice Cream Man

John Tait was descended from generations of miners, firstly in the lead mines of Alston and then in the coal mines of Northumberland. His grandfather was killed in Mickley Coke Works in 1870.

He was born in Haltwhistle the son of coal miner Thomas Tait and his wife Margaret Ann (née Eals) in 1903. He was the fourth child in a family of seven.

His mother died when he was ten years old and he was brought up by his Granny Eals, a widow, along with about twelve other children. Times were very hard as the First World War was about to starts so the granny was forced to take in lodgers to make ends meet. She also had a little shop in her back kitchen, selling sweets to the local children and using any profit to feed her extended family. It was this that might have attracted John to be a shopkeeper in later life.

After leaving elementary school

John Tait.

at twelve years of age he followed his father to become a boy miner, in the South Tyne Colliery, Haltwhistle, his wages going to his granny to help feed the family, as was the custom in those days. During his schooldays and in his teens he was a very keen boy scout.

When he was eighteen the colliery closed down and he had to leave home to find work, as his granny could not afford to feed him without his wages coming in. He went live with and work for his uncle, who was Italian, and owned a confectionery and ice cream shop in Hebburn. His uncle came from a family of ice cream makers in Italy, and he passed on his recipes and skills to John. While he worked for his uncle, he met and became friendly with Dolly Pavani, who was in England, working as a servant for another Italian family in Newcastle.

As time went by his uncle's business became less profitable and he could no longer employ John. At the same time Dolly's contract was up and she was packed to go to join her family. Her family had left Italy and moved to Paris. She did not relish the idea of going to a new country and learning a new language. John said to her that they should get married and face the uncertain future together, and that's what they did. John went to live with his brother George at Blyth and Dolly stayed with a neighbour, and they were married on 15th December 1923.

As newly weds, both only twenty years of age and with nowhere to live they had to live in lodgings in Blyth while they looked for work. John managed to find work as a labourer on Blyth harbour walls. When the walls were completed he found another job as a miner at Choppington High Pit. He had to walk from Blyth to work and back, which took him two hours each way. He would often call at a shop at Scotland Gate on his way to or from work and became friendly with the owner Dominic Colonel who was also an Italian. Dominic offered to give Dolly a job, so she used to walk from Blyth with her husband and back again when he finished his shift at the pit. Soon they were accompanied by little Stanley in his pram.

This arrangement lasted until 1926 when Dominic went bankrupt as a result of the 1926 Strike and the shop was closed down. John continued to pass the shop on his way to work for the next two years and he decided to have a go at being a shopkeeper. He borrowed £5 to move to what was by now an almost derelict property. For several months they and their three children slept on the floor while they made the house habitable and the shop fit to open. To make some money in the meantime John hawked the local villages selling clippings for mat making, a popular cottage industry at that time. In due course the hard working couple opened the shop and became popular with the locals who identified with John who had worked with them in the pit.

The shop had been a Social Club during the war, it was popularly known as 'The Pig and Whistle' and there was a large cellar attached. As the business prospered, John bought equipment to make ice cream and installed it in the cellar. He was then able to practice those skills he had learnt from his uncle at Hebburn.

The ice cream was of high quality and business boomed, and soon he was employing several people to sell ice cream from horse and carts, tricycles, and motor vans. As he prospered he did not forget his many relatives in Haltwhistle, and he often went there laden with sweets and foodstuff from the shop which he gave to them. Some of his cousins came to work for him in the summertime. He also provided furnishings and money for churches of all denominations in the town. The Boy Scouts and other youth organisations also benefited from his generosity. Similar groups in Choppington were given help.

In the late 1930s John bought three ice cream shops which at that time were known as Temperance Bars. They were situated at Ashington, North Seaton and Bedlington. His intention was to eventually to have a shop for each for his five children, which they would then pass on to his grandchildren. At that point his ambitions came to a full stop when the Second World War began and he was called up to serve in the Royal Air Force. Ice cream was not allowed to be made, and sweets, chocolate, and food was rationed. How was the business to survive? His wife had five children to look after and the future looked bleak.

Dolly proved to be the saviour of enterprise. She had been abandoned as a new born baby on the steps of a hospital in Rome, and was fostered by a large family. She was not sent to school and spent most of her childhood working on the land. She came to England to work, which was an act of great courage in itself, to escape from the mundane life in Italy. Her strength and experiences stood her in good stead and she cheerfully embraced the responsibilities of running the business while John went to war. She was assisted by her two eldest children Stan and Irene. Stan had volunteered to be a Bevan Boy to work in the local pit so that he could stay at home and help his mother between shifts. To save the shops they sold peas and pies, Oxo, teas and Spam sandwiches, which was very popular with their customers as food was scarce. Many local people helped the family through difficult times, which was much appreciated, and John never forgot what they did to help. As a token of his appreciation he helped many people when they were in difficulties, and indeed several local businesses were launched with financial help from John Tait.

After the war John returned home to run the business, with his wife who was as able as him to take business decisions. Once again the manufacture of ice cream was resumed under the auspices of the eldest son Stan, who had been taught the craft from his father. The demand for Tait's ice cream grew and a modern ice cream factory was built in 1947 behind the shop at Choppington. Each year Diplomas were awarded for the quality of the product at the National Ice Cream competitions. The family inherited their parents' capacity for hard work and he used to tell his friends how proud he was of them.

In the late 1940s three of John's friends were killed in separate accidents at Choppington Colliery and he wanted to have a memorial in the church for them. He presented a processional cross which was dedicated to all the men who had lost their lives at Choppington Colliery.

The 1950s saw the business grow again with several ice cream vans operating in the area bordered by Blyth, Amble, Alnwick, and Morpeth. John was never happier than to be serving at the ice cream kiosk near the riverside and park at Morpeth. In the late 1950s he began to suffer from ill health so he fulfilled his ambitions by transferring the business to his family. The shop at Ashington went to Stan, the one at Bedlington to Irene, the North Seaton one to Audrey, and the one at Choppington to David and Alan. The ice cream factory and vans were given to Stan, David, and son-in-law Jack Ricalton.

John was then able to enjoy a few years in semi retirement and enjoyed himself by spending extended holidays with friends in Belgium, France, and Italy.

John Tait died in January 1963, and his wife Dolly died in June 1964.

David Tait
Bedlington, 2001

Philanthropist, John Tait, presents a bowling trophy at Morpeth. Councillor Alfred Appleby is third from the left.

The Musical Millicans

Alan Millican and Tommy Nesbitt brought fame to Bedlingtonshire with their success on Hughie Green's TV programme, 'Opportunity Knocks' in the 1970s. They followed this up by topping variety bills throughout the country for a few years before quitting the big-time.

It all started for the Millican family at North Row, West Sleekburn when the Millican brothers would stand outside on a fine night and sing in harmony to anybody who wanted to listen. This progressed to a sextet being formed with Bob, Alan and Derek Millican, Tommy Nesbitt and his cousin Raymond Nesbitt. Ken Smith was the other member who sang professionally as 'The Sextet' for many years.

Bob Millican, Jack Allen and Alan Hetherington formed a trio famous for its skiffle music. This was in the middle and late 1950s when Lonnie Donegan was scraping his washboard.

The Millican and Nesbitt families gather together at the peak of Tommy and Alan's popularity.

From the 1950s until recent years the Tubby twins (Betty and Babs) entertained all age groups with their excellent singing. There isn't a local concert, men's or women's group they haven't entertained over the years. The 'Fret' at Stakeford often had concerts and Betty and Babs would be there. They performed on Frank Wappat's Radio Newcastle show and were well known all over the Newcastle and Northumberland areas.

You had to be some player to represent England as a schoolboy footballer, yet Jimmy Middlemass of Guide Post Secondary School did just that in 1949. This was a great honour for Jimmy of course and the school, whose headmaster, Mr W. Morgan, was Chairman of the English Schools FA at the time. Jimmy played for England schoolboys at left full back with Duncan Edwards and David Pegg (later of Manchester United). He signed for Newcastle United and played regularly for Newcastle Juniors (The N's) and the reserve side, but an injury saw him leave St James' Park to see out his career at Ashington in the North Eastern League. It is no coincidence that his piece about Jimmy is next to the Tubby sisters item; Betty and Jimmy married in 1952 and now have two daughters and four grandchildren.

A Long Police Connection

A remarkable link with the police force in Bedlington goes back to the early 1920s when Sgt James Taylor was resident sergeant at the old police station at the top of the town. His son, Tom Taylor, followed in father's footsteps then grandson Jim Robinson in 1962, after eight years as a fitter at the 'Aad' pit, joined the West Riding Police Force, moving through the ranks of uniform and CID to finish inspector with the Northumbrian force in 1992.

Many will remember Jim's dad, Ted Robinson, well known insurance rep and Jim's grandmother Frances, who was licensee at 'The Grapes' for many years.

Right: Sgt James Taylor and his wife, Suzannah.

Jim Robinson and Norman Craigs on bank at Bedlington 'A' Pit.

She Came, She Saw, She Wanted To Stay

About six years ago, it was a particularly nice summer's afternoon so I decided to have a bit dig in my back garden in Bedlington Station. I became aware of a couple leaning on my fence, looking straight at me. The woman was red-faced, lips quivering and trying hard not to cry. 'Auntie Edna?' she asked.

'Well I'm Edna, but I don't think I'm your Auntie,' was my answer.

'I'm Shirley, Shirley Laws, and I haven't seen you for over fifty years.'

I realised after a few seconds shock, that this grown up woman of sixty years was the young girl I'd had for six years as an evacuee from North London.

My mind was taken back to the beginning of the war in 1939 when I was asked to take Shirley into my home in Wilson Avenue, East Sleekburn.

It didn't take long for me to agree to take on the eleven year old as company for my two kids, Edna and Robert. Her mother wrote to me and told me she would put Shirley on a train at King's Cross and I would know her at the Central Station as she would be wearing a black velour hat, bright red coat and would carry a rag doll.

Shirley was spotted straight away. What her mother forgot to mention was her beautiful blonde ringlets flowing down onto her shoulders.

Shirley Laws on right with her husband and Edna Halligan senior and junior.

Shirley loved East Sleekburn and Cambois straight away. She quickly made friends, learned the lingo and settled into school.

Over the years I had to be careful not to get too attached. I realised she wasn't mine and she would one day return to her natural parents and home in London.

When the fateful day arrived in 1945, Shirley didn't want to leave us. She was a Northumbrian, a Cambois one at that. She was a teenager with many connections here, but a very sensible girl too.

Shirley's mother came to collect her and amidst tears and blubbering farewells, she went back to London and I never saw her again, until that emotional day in my back garden six years ago.

She was with her husband and seemed perfectly happy. Somehow, though, if somebody had said you can stay in Bedlingtonshire, I feel she wouldn't have to be asked twice.

Edna Halligan
Sleekburn, 2001

'Sisters, Sisters. There Were Never Such Devoted Sisters'

An event I looked forward to as a kid was the night mother and her four sisters got together for sandwiches, cakes and slaggings off. Their husbands would accompany them, taking a back seat with caps on their knees while the wives held forth around the front room table, hats pinned to the hair and handbags at the feet. They would condescend to remove coats which is just as well as the fire was double banked with best coal.

I can only recount events at our house as I only once ventured to a Bedlington sister's (Aunt Lil). Aunt Lil was the organist in the family and she would change the tempo after the food with renditions on her Minnesota American pedal organ of various Sankey & Moody hymns, from her Primitive Methodist collection. It was forever one, to be better than the other. Aunt Mary Ann, the oldest sister, always took the responsibility of checking the sandwiches before consuming. 'Aa see yiv got red salmon wor Lil. Aa hope it's John West's. Aa divvent care for the stuff wi had once ower at somebody's aal not mention. Aa swear it was Store paste.'

The September get-together guaranteed one-upmanship about holidays. By the early 1950s, Aunt Jinny and Uncle Jack had 'progressed' over the Pennines to Morecambe from Skeggy. The 'hotel' (glorified boarding house) was the next best thing to the Savoy according to Aunt Jinny. She was the leader of the pack and nobody could emulate her although Lil and Ethel tried their best.

'The eggs were massive, wornt they Jack?'

'Yis Jinny they war,' Uncle Jack ascented.

'And the manageress telt wi, wi cud hev an extra slice of bacon. Didn't shi Jack?'

'Yis shi did, Jinny Hinny,' a nod of the head endorsing.

All this was relayed by Jinny without a turn of the head or glance at Jack behind her. God only knows what fate would have befallen Uncle Jack if he hadn't agreed.

The sisters all had pet names used by the others, but should any sign of contradiction arise they were given the names Grannie Neave had them Christened with. Al became Alice, Ett – Ethel, Jinny – Jane, Lil – Eliza and wor Mare – Mary Ann.

They were all good living, God fearing ladies. Their husbands had these qualities too, touched, thank goodness, with more than a dab of tolerance.

The Neave family in 1907. Bill and Sarah with their children Mary Ann (the oldest) Bill Junior, Jean, Eliza and baby Alice. Ethel was born two years later.

A Night In The Cree

Mother (Alice) and Auntie Mary Ann were the quiet ones of the five sisters and both were very deaf without their Peacock of Grey Street's hearing aid. Mary Ann got her's first in about 1947 and mother followed the next year. Before they acquired these major benefits to life, both Dad and Uncle George made signs and the ladies lip-read a lot.

Dad filled a lot of his spare time in his allotment behind Milburn

Terrace and many summer nights were spent gardening and 'gassing' there until darkness set in.

One night I was spending a night at my godmother's (Aunt Jinnie) house in Bedlington. This was just after the war and the consequence of my absence and mother's deafness left my dad trapped for four hours in the backyard cree. In West and East Terraces, everybody had a back yard which included the coalhouse, netty and cree. Dad had his 5 o'clock dinner after work and motioned to my mother that he was going to the allotment. She nodded. Dad disappeared and five minutes later Mam went across the yard to the loo, saw the cree door open and banged it shut before disappearing into the toilet. Dad of course was inside gathering his garden gear. No matter how he yelled and shouted no one could hear him. It wasn't until 10.30 that Tommy Smailes, next door, came into his yard, heard Dad's yells and asked the obvious question 'Is that ee Stephen? Where are yi?'

Tom rescued my old man by lifting the cree sneck and a disgruntled father crossed the yard and into the house to be greeted by a nightgowned and Dinkie curlered Ma. 'Did ye get yer leeks in Stephen? There's yer Horlicks on the kitchen table.'

Colliery Wives

My mother and all her sisters were colliery wives and followed the traditions and working patterns of their mother before them. It wasn't always the case with colliery ladies, but my female relations had the full pay packets, plus overtime bonuses paid up to them on a Friday. No 'keepy-backs' with the Neave women.

Old Gannie Threadgold up the street had five sons who all worked at the pit and she ran a meticulously clean house with a rod of iron.

She had the build of a heavyweight boxer with arms, it seems, permanently folded under a huge bosom. Tommy Smailes described this perfectly by saying she was 'Timmad reet up t' th' fyes.'

We lads playing 'Door Kickee' football in the back lane with a small ball, would draw lots if the ball went into Gannie's yard.

Always, she was too quick for us. She'd see the ball arrive in her yard, wait, watching behind the kitchen curtain, until the poor 'short strawer' raced onto her premises. Then all nineteen stones of her would appear with a few selected expressions of rage and antipathy to harangue our comrade, forever finishing with her famed demand: 'Geddaway back t' yer owen hooses. Aam keepin' ya baal ye maaks (maggots).'

Many years later I met the girl who was to become my wife and I was persuaded to visit her great aunt, at St John's Place, Bedlington Station for tea one Sunday afternoon.

A new expression was created for faces when Aunt Mary was none other than Gannie Threadgold. She must have known who Judith's new boyfriend was and her eyes twinkled as she greeted me with 'Hev ye cum fo' ya baal, ye little maak?'

St John's Church at Bedlington Station. Auntie Mary lived just behind here.
Miss Easton was the great patron of St John's Church.

Rev B.W. Taylor, Vicar of St John's.

SECTION FOUR

SPORTING TIMES

Newcastle United has always been famous for its Number 9s. Here is Vic Keeble in action in the 1950s.

Supporting The Toon

It was just after the war when I first went to St James' Park. Tommy and Eliza, next door, fanatical Sunderland supporters, had already had me at Roker Park to see Manchester City and the great Frank Swift. I'd enjoyed that, but no way was my father going to let me be a red and white. His father, also Stephen, had seen United's first match in 1892 and my dad never missed a home match.

Newcastle's mascot from the 1950s.

A local newspaper cartoon published after Newcastle's first League game against old rivals, Sunderland in 1898.

My first match in 1946 saw Newcastle draw 1-1 with Swansea Town. I clearly remember Jimmy Woodburn was our marksman, converting a Tommy Pearson cross. Tommy Swinburne was Newcastle's keeper. I sat on a barrier at the Leazes End and felt this isn't a bad way to spend a Saturday afternoon. The alternative was shopping up Northumberland Street with mother and Aunt Lil.

I quickly became addicted and eventually joined the bus from the Rowton every other Saturday. Sixpence got me there and back to join the regular crowds of 50,000 plus, although you had to be there early to be guaranteed a seat on the wall at the front of the 'Popular' side. Being late generally meant being heaved down the terraces over heads; an experience I had once and never wanted again.

The peanut man was popular, 'Peanuts, tanner a bag!' was his cry and no matter how far back in the crowd the purchaser was, he was directly hit by the Geordie lad selling the nuts.

If the game was awful, and the Toon in no way looking like winners, the ten minute flag at the corner of the Gallowgate signalled a mass

United's team of the early 1950s. Back row: Bobby Cowell, Joe Harvey, Jack Fairbrother, Tot Smith, Alf McMichael, Charlie Crowe. Front row: Bobby Mitchell, Tommy Walker, Ernie Taylor, Jackie Milburn, George Robledo.

exodus. This saved waiting until the finish and being 'carried' down the exit stairs by the mass of bodies.

I occasionally regretted leaving early, no more so than when Newcastle were 1-2 down in a cup-tie with ten minutes to go in 1952, against Aston Villa, only for Bobby Mitchell especially, and Jackie to turn on the magic and the Gallowgate roar sucked the ball into that end's net for United to win 4-2.

United On TV

I watched the 1952 FA cup final on a hazy-screen television. The transmitter was in Holme-Moss, South Yorkshire and the reception was very poor. By 1955 we had Pontop Pike sending out signals and the Toon were at Wembley again, playing Manchester City. We had the house full of neighbours and relations and two of my cousins had their tiny babies with them. In the first minute Jackie headed in from a corner. It was unheard of for Jackie to head the ball and I jumped up, shouted 'goal' and woke up the babies – and there was hell on. They had to take the babies out and shove dummies in their mouths to keep them quiet.

Memorable Players

Looking back on my St James' days and wishing we could have some of the long gone players with us now. I crave for a Ronnie Simpson in goal and a Frank Brennan in the centre of defence.

I enjoy Newcastle going forward and think the present squad has possibilities, but the aforementioned two might give us more command of the penalty area.

Simpson wasn't a big lad, but he dominated the box as did big Frank. I only every saw him turned over once at St James' Park and that was by equally large Derek Dooley of Sheffield Wednesday who was quicker on the turn.

The most entertaining Newcastle player I've seen in 55 years of supporting is Peter Beardsley. He could turn a game with one piece of magic. Closely following Peter is Tony Green who we signed from Blackpool, but he only played for us a short while, then was injured to play no more.

Jackie Milburn, Malcolm MacDonald, Gazza, Chris Waddle, even Barrie Thomas, added thousands to the gate in their time and Ivor Allchurch was the classic old fashioned inside forward.

Peter Beardsley and Paul Gascoigne. Two local lads whose extraordinary talent made them household names. 50,000 Toon supporters wish we had them at their peak today.

In later years, when working for Radio Newcastle, I had the good fortune (mostly) to meet players of the past and present. One of the nicest guys I spent an evening with at St James' Park was the very modest, unassuming but tremendous centre forward, Len White. He was up there with Newcastle's best ever players, yet came to St James' from Rotherham as a second choice right winger. He got his chance at centre forward and never looked back. It was a disgrace that he never made the full England side but always played well for the Football League with the great Johnny Haynes of Fulham his provider.

Having mentioned these outstanding players, and hopefully jogged the memories of football fanatics, I look at the present squad and think we've at least one who ranks with the greats. Keiron Dyer is a wonderful player, of world-class. I sincerely hope he keeps his word and stays with the black and whites for a long time to come.

Radio Times

When I got to the age when even walking pace five-a-side football was impossible, I looked for some other form of 'hands on' participation with sport and it came in the form of football, mainly, and other sports broadcasts throughout each year.

Working for BBC Radio Newcastle was a treat. I'd already done my radio apprenticeship with Radio Tyneside Hospitals Broadcasts doing regular commentaries from St James' Park.

Jim Harland, Sports Producer at Crestina House, asked me to work part-time for his sports department, doing a variety of sports commentaries. I spent the next twelve years achieving another boyhood ambition travelling to most of the big soccer grounds covering Newcastle, Sunderland and Middlesboro, with Carlisle, Hartlepool and Darlington thrown in for good measure.

BBC Radio Newcastle were always keen to cover Athletics in the area and Stan Long, Brendon Foster's coach, was our expert. It was an event Stan and I were covering that nearly brought an end to my career. It was Boxing Day 1983 and the two of us were sent to a farm in County Durham to cover a cross-country championship. The ground was knee deep in clarts and unfortunately it was through this quagmire we had to take the BBC radio car to our vantage point up a hillside. Stan was against the idea of attempting the climb, but I knew we would never get a signal from the studio unless we were 'up top'. Anyway, we could only view the race from there. What I hadn't thought about was the surfeit of mud, filthy water and flotsam the radio car would throw up.

The decision was made. We'd attempt the drive up. I decided, as driver, to race 20 yards to the bottom of the hill and hopefully the four-wheel drive would get us the 30 yards or so to the summit.

Stan was hanging on, white knuckled as we made our way, mostly sideways, when suddenly there appeared on the side of the hill, a startled woman with her hands in the air shouting 'No, No, No-o-o.'

Too late the deed was done. She had been the most elegantly dressed spectator there. Her husband had bought her for Christmas, the most tasteful light blue suede coat, edged in fur, with matching hat, handbag and knee length boots. Within seconds she was like Al Jolsen, only the eyeballs showing any white. To say she and her husband were upset would be playing the soft pedal. After the husband's roaring and the woman's interpretation of the Haka, I suggested they send a bill to the BBC for the necessary cleaning job.

Stan and I covered the event and we went back to the studio where producer Jim had been earbashed by the couple. I was given a ticking off and I suspect, although it was never confirmed, that the BBC forked out for a new outfit as the 'cleaning', not surprisingly, had proved unsuccessful.

Sorry Dennis

Sunderland weren't ever my favourite side, although I tried to be impartial when covering their matches and genuinely liked all North East sides to do well. One game in the late 1980s at Roker saw Sunderland leading 2-0 in an important promotion game at home to Oldham, to end up on the wrong end of a 3-2 scoreline. Denis Smith, the manager must have been a mixture of mad, disappointed, humiliated and frustrated. All greenhorn reporters take note. Never ask any coach or manager the question I put to Denis at our after match radio interview. It was, 'Are you disappointed Denis?'

He went ballistic and fortunately for him, me and the listeners, his rhetoric was taped, not live and was never played.

Denis Smith (a good guy) never spoke to me again.

Losing Count

Never try commentating on swimming events unless you have a helper. My experience at the Dunston Baths is in the sports annals at Radio Newcastle. I had to cover a free style event over 25 laps of the pool. The race was a none-event as English international Janet White was too much of a challenge for her novice opponents. Working alone I had numbered 1 to 25 on paper and as the leader touched and turned, I ticked off each lap. Unfortunately in trying to make this drab contest interesting I was trying to cover all six girls in various positions in the race.

Looking at my paper I'd ticked off 24 laps and so, with a mouthful of false confidence, I pronounced, 'Here is Janet White, showing her full international class, leaving her opponents in her slipstream to touch now to comfortably win the race.'

To my horror Janet touched and turned again as she'd only completed 24 laps. I couldn't think of anything constructive to say but

left the immortal words on tape, 'Would you believe it, Janet is doing another lap. Never mind she's so far ahead she'll win at half pace.'
  I never lived that one down.

Not Everything Is As It Sounds

BBC Radio Newcastle was always keen to promote its programmes by doing good turns for local clubs and organisations. The sports team flew its flag by organising sports quizzes across the area, providing small prizes as well as entertainment. It never failed to amaze me, how some lads and lasses had the most infinite knowledge of a sport, which meant a retentive mind, yet worked as electricians, builders, labourers, etc.
  One particular night in early Autumn 1978 is worth recounting. One of the news team, Joss, recently appointed to the area from the

Denis Smith in goal for Stoke City against Everton in 1969. Denis' regular position was centre half but during this game Stoke's goalkeeper had been injured. In the days before substitute goalies, Denis took over the 'keeper's jersey. Everton eventually ran out 6-2 winners.

Midlands, volunteered to organize a sports quiz at Newbiggin. This was mainly to learn about the geography and people of the area, to which he was a newcomer.

Jim Harland provided Joss with his questions and answers, pencils, clock and small blackboard on which to record the scores. A roughly drawn map was given, leading him to the spine road and eventually Newbiggin across the Kitty Brewster bridge.

Joss had a small roof rack on his vehicle and to this he fastened his blackboard with two elasticated straps.

The evening was fine, but very windy and there were sudden violent gusts on parts of the open road. Joss reached the Three Horse Shoes area at Horton with little trouble, and headed for the Kitty Brewster bridge. Halfway down that particular part of road, a violent rush of wind took the blackboard off its straps and into the nearside field.

Joss was naturally alarmed by this as he had signed the BBC blackboard out and was responsible for it and how was he going to keep the score?

The blackboard had landed in an overgrown meadow and there was no sight of it. Joss walked up and down the fenced paddock with little hope of success when down the road came a Sleekburn worthy, giving his dog some exercise.

'Hev yi lost sumthin marra?' was the query.

'Yes,' replied Joss. 'A blackboard. You haven't come across one have you?'

'No hinny.' Was the answer. 'But Aa've seen two spuggies and a pigeon doon the road if they're any gud.'

Joss never found his blackboard, but he continued on to Newbiggin for a successful quiz show. He being a wiser man about our feathered friends and how their names should be pronounced.

SECTION FIVE

OTHER TALES

One of the funniest sights in the rows just after the war, was of Harry Crawford riding his motor bike. Many men would do this but few would equal Harry's exploits on a sunny afternoon in 1947.

Harry had no idea of how to ride a motor bike. His only experience of two wheel riding was his Milne Major pedal cycle, which he'd bought before the war. He'd always envied Bob Hamer his Velocette MOV 250cc bike and when Bob decided to sell, Harry was there like a shot. £15 changed hands and Harry was mounted and away to the wobbliest of starts. His Jackson the Tailor's cap was back to front and fortunately for Harry and pedestrians, he was in a permanent second gear with no idea how to accelerate or to stop the machine. Consequently he made at least twenty four trips to the top of the street and round the back lane until the petrol ran out, thus ending the adventure.

Harry's exploit had managed to empty most of the houses onto the street, some hanging out their upstairs windows, waving as he passed. The story proved good enough for the *Blyth News*, who printed the tale in their weekly newspaper.

An Early School In Bedlingtonshire

Michael Longridge of Bedlington Ironworks, encouraged his workmen to have their children educated. His school, established in 1821, down the Free Wood, provided the teaching of Reading, Writing, Arithmetic, Knitting and Sewing. Writing in 1842 he, 'lamented that the parents have not availed themselves of the school as they should have done. Perhaps this may be attributed to them paying too little towards its support. We charge the unmarried men 1d per week, and the married men 2d per week. Out of this fund, we defer the expense of the school; books etc, salary to a schoolmaster and mistress, and provide our workmen and their families with medical attendance and medicine.

The parents find the cost of education so very low, estimate its value very low and do not care whether their children attend or not. An Infants' school has been lately established. Sunday Schools are taught at the works, and the village and an Evening School is likewise kept.

Several of the older apprentices in the engine factory are taught drawing, and for this they pay 6d per week.'

The children's school in 1842, had 50 girls and the same number of boys, 5 years and older. They were taught 30 hours per week and the method used was 'interrogatory and explanatory.'

These gargoyles were in the ironworks school yard in the Free Wood. They were of some religious significance and remained there until the site was razed about 30 years ago.

Life With Harry Dobson At Choppington Junior School

The year after my arrival at Choppington Junior School I was given full responsibility of the football team and having no soccer background, I was obliged to purchase a book on the rules, which I studied long and carefully, as I was expected to referee all home games.

So terrified was I, at this daunting prospect, I often resorted to the dubious, not to say dishonest, ploy of bandaging an ankle or knee, thus feigning an injury and then pleading with the master-in-charge of the visiting team to referee in my stead.

On one particular Wednesday, we were entertaining one of the Ashington schools (who at that time had a stranglehold on success in all the cups and trophies available, and had done for many years) and whose headmaster was a qualified referee who had actually officiated at Wembley, no less. I told him of my 'injury' and he gladly agreed to take my place.

Twenty or thirty local dads lined the touchlines as the game kicked off. Being a Wednesday and Market Day in nearby Morpeth, a number of them had spent the entire afternoon in the town's public houses and several of them were 'rather the worse for wear'.

The game proceeded and, as was the agreed custom the referee offered the occasional criticism and encouragement to the players on both sides – quite impartially. However, those 'in their cups' took exception to the ref's behaviour and believed he was favouring his own team. The mood among spectators was growing decidedly unpleasant and the language decidedly more 'colourful'. We lost the game and when the final whistle blew, two or three particularly incensed fathers were determined to 'have the ref'.

I had quickly to rush both him and his lads from the field to the sanctuary of the school hall, bolting the outer doors as a precaution. To say the referee was shaken and upset, would be an understatement. The angry, inebriated dads were shaking the porch doors, violently, and bellowing their threats in strong Anglo-Saxon language. I went outside to try and pacify them and after a while they reluctantly wandered off home. When the coast was finally clear the Ashington contingent left the building to catch their bus. The headmaster swore he would never again, under any circumstances, referee a game at Choppington – and he never did.

But shortly after, the iron grip the Hirst schools had enjoyed on league and cup successes, was finally broken and for four or five wonderful years, Choppington at long last, found its 'place in the sun.'

Natural Nature Study

'Nature Study' in the '60s was still considered an integral part of the curriculum and could, depending on the teacher's knowledge, empathy and enthusiasm for the subject, excite the interest in the children.

A young Harry Dobson and headmaster 'Mac' Brown with their 1961-62 trophy winning side.

As part of their studies, one of my classes, was set the task of collecting100 different wild flowers – which, later, in class they would have to press, identify, categorise and so on.

There seemed a genuine enthusiasm on their part as many of the children lived in areas where there were plenty of 'wild' green areas.

We were in the middle of discussing the project when suddenly, from the back of the room, a low voice growled – 'I'm not collecting any bloody flowers.' You could have heard a pin drop.

Immediately, identifying the source of this unexpected and colourful outburst as from my school goalkeeper I challenged him – 'What did you say?'

'I'm not collecting any bloody flowers,' he repeated – nothing abashed.

To be fair to the lad he wasn't intending to be cheeky or to provoke me: he was simply, in his own way, issuing a statement of fact in language, which, to him, was commonplace, and he had no idea that 'that word' simply was not used in 'polite society'.

Normally, he was a very quiet sort of lad: he never caused trouble and he never got into any. Nevertheless, I couldn't turn a deaf ear to this kind of language being used in my classroom – and by a ten-year-old.

'Come out here, at once,' I instructed; but R— wasn't having any. Before I could grab him he was up out of his desk; he darted out the door, dashed down the corridor and out of the porch as fast as his legs would take him. He lived only a few hundred yards from the school and returned about an hour later, just as the children were coming into school from their morning break. I was standing framed in my classroom doorway. I seized him by the collar as he attempted (totally unconcerned) to enter the room.

'And where have you been?' I asked him.

'Home,' was his instant reply.

'Did you tell your mother what you had said to me?' I enquired.

He mumbled his reply in the affirmative.

'And what did she say?' I persisted.

'She said I shouldn't have been so rude and that I should say I'm sorry,' was the answer.

'Rude, rude!' I exploded. 'I might hear language like that on a building site but I do not expect to hear it in my classroom.'

What more could I say and to be honest I had some difficulty hiding my smile. The laddie simply had no idea he'd caused any offence. It was a word he was used to hearing and he had used it as he would any other.

Punishment was out of the question. I had threatened his 'street cred' (though the term was still to be coined). Imagine his mates seeing him coming down the street with a bunch of wood anemones and primroses – he would never have been able to hold his head up high again, ever!

In any case, he broke his finger playing in a football practice a fortnight later and I had to take him to Ashington Hospital to have it reset which, after he came out of the anaesthetic left him in more than a little discomfort. Perhaps this was some kind of 'Divine retribution' though, by now, our normally friendly relationship had been totally restored and the incident of the flowers had been completely forgotten.

I had the immense good fortune, when I began my teaching career at Choppington; to work for a headmaster whom I thought was 'the bees knees'.

He was a wonderful man, kind, tolerant and understanding – and he knew just how to handle a callow fellow who wanted to put the world to rights, and who knew just how to do it ... or so I deluded myself.

I honestly believed school holidays were a 'pain in the bum' since they interrupted what I really wanted to do, which was to teach seven days a week.

One of the things I did with 'my lads' (entirely with 'Mac's' approval) was to send them (unaccompanied) cross-country running.

They would start in the Welfare Park at Scotland Gate, skirt the bottom of the 'pit-heap', make their way past the 'pond' until they reached the lonnen that brought them out on the Guide Post – Morpeth main road at Clark's farm.

I would meet them at the farm and escort them down the road to the Guide Post corner where they assembled prior to their returning down the road to Scotland Gate and thus back (safely) to school.

On one of these occasions one of the lads had strayed rather too close to the edge of the 'pit pond' and fell into the 'sleck'.

Eventually arriving back at school he was, literally, covered from head to feet (inclusively) in grey slime.

All we could do, was to stand him in two handbasins, in the porch, borrow a large jug from the kitchen and douse him in warm water from head to foot.

We dried him with paper towels and left him probably cleaner than he was before we started, and none the worse for his experience.

'Mac' might have taken me to task for what had happened but he did not. He accepted the incident for what it was – an accident; nor did he say that the runs had to stop. But no way today in the present climate would any young gamesmaster be allowed the freedom I was given. It was a different age and it has gone forever.

I thank God for those wonderful years and bless the memory of 'Mac' Brown, a man for whom (with every member of his staff) I had the greatest respect and affection – it was a privilege and pleasure to serve under him.

Harry G. Dobson
Morpeth, 2001

What Are Wellies For Anyway?

In the days when the local vicar and schoolmaster were looked up to, Bedlington Station School had a man, Mr Boundy, who was highly respected in the village. He was head of the school for a number of years before and after the Second World War.

Apparently he wasn't the sort of person who would readily tell tales out of school, but he recounted a story to a member of his staff Mary Crow, who entertained a party after chapel one night with its telling.

Mr Boundy had been taking in, on a part time basis, youngsters from West Sleekburn. The head of that school had informed him that they were being 'decanted'. This was a word the County Office had invented for children being farmed out to a neighbouring school for a short period of time. Apparently some alterations were being done to West Sleekburn houses and instead of moving families into caravans, they were being 'decanted' into empty Bedlington Station properties.

Generally the children stayed for six to eight weeks, not really enough time to become settled and they were usually happy when they could return home.

In the middle of this to-ing and fro-ing, Mr Boundy made the children and parents from across the fields welcome and apart from the odd abrasive face to face, the situation was passing over satisfactorily.

Then one Monday morning a harassed looking mother appeared at Boundy's office door. 'Are ee the heedmaster?' she asked.

Boundy assented with a nod and welcoming handshake.

'Aam Mrs Broon from the Winnin' and am settin' wor Ronnie doon here 'til wi get shifted back. Mind e's the softest laddy i' the Winnin'

64

school and am worried t' deeth aboot 'im comin' here in case 'e gets bullied.'

Mr Boundy assured the mother there would be no bullying, but taking one look at 'Wor Ronnie' he wondered how long it would be before his personal appearance would be questioned by some of the Station hard lads. Looking at Ronnie, the headmaster conjured up visions of Jimmy James' side-kick, Eli, who often played the Newcastle Empire and indeed had performed at the Station's Palace Theatre in his early days.

Boundy's plan to save this lad from certain humiliation was to get the school hardman, Jimmy Tyas, to protect Ronnie and be his pal in the relatively short time he was with them.

After bidding Mrs Brown farewell, Jimmy Tyas was summoned to the head's office, which wasn't an unusual occurrence as most of the school yard aggro emanated from Jimmy and his marras.

'Hello, Mr Boundy, waat hev a done?'

'Nothing, Jimmy.' The head assured him. 'I've got a job for you.'

'Fo' me?' an astounded Jimmy replied. 'Do aa get a toffee chew like the milk monitors?' future union man Jimmy enquired.

'If you do the job properly Jimmy, You'll get a packet of toffee chews at the end of the job.' Promised the headmaster.

Jimmy's eyes were rolling at the prospect of getting in with the boss and having sweeties at the end of it all.

Then came the discussion around the practical details of the task. 'What's the job like Sor?' Jimmy was told his mission and introduced to a petrified Ronnie who was looked up and down by his new pal.

Mr Boundy with one of his school classes, in his first year at Bedlington Station in 1926.

'When do Aa start?' Boundy was asked.

'This playtime and every playtime and dinner time from then on. I'll be watching out for you.'

The days went by and the head's plan was working a treat. The thought of the toffee chews packet at the end of his assignment meant Jimmy paraded around the school with an arm around Ronnie's shoulders to show his dedication to the job.

Meanwhile the staff had noticed Ronnie had large wellie boots on every day which he refused to take off. Mary Crow had actually taken a PE lesson where Ronnie had done a vault over the PE horse where his size 4 wellies had landed before him and somehow his size 2 feet had touched down inside the wellies shortly after.

At a staff meeting two or three weeks after Ronnie's arrival, the Any Other Business section dwelt upon the 'decantees' in general and Ronnie Broon in particular. His wellies were mentioned and the head was reminded of Mrs Brown's parting shot as she left the building that first morning: 'Mind, wor Ronnie'll not tyek them wellies off. His gannie bowt them for Christmas and 'e gans t' bed wi them on.'

Not wanting to disrupt the Jimmy, Ronnie, Boundy triangular project, the headmaster persuaded his staff to put up with Ronnie's wellie foible for the sake of peace and quiet.

By the beginning of the sixth week there were signs that Jimmy was getting a bit tired of the Ronnie alliance, although there were no complaints from the Browns and things were left to take a natural course.

On the Thursday of Ronnie's last week, staff noticed that Jimmy was nowhere near Ronnie and had obviously given up his protection racket for the time being. Then at the lunchtime Meggie Dodds, the dinner woman, knocked on the staffroom door with a wellie clad, worried looking Ronnie by her side.

What is the problem Mrs Dodds?' Mr Boundy asked.

'Ee's plodgin' in ees wellies,' was Meggie's reply.

'But it's a fine sunny day. There's no water to plodge in,' observed Mr Boundy.

'The wettors inside ees wellies,' said Meggie.

'Inside his wellingtons?' came the echo. 'How's the water got inside his wellingtons?'

Meggie's statement was down to earth. 'Am not tellin' yi. Am a Rechabite, but waat his muther'll think when ee gets back, I do not know. Yill hev t' ask him hoo ee got wettor in ees wellies.'

At that point Mr Boundy turned to the feckless Ronnie and asked pointedly: 'How has the water got into your wellies Ronnie?'

Without a second's hesitation Ronnie told him: 'Jimmy Tyas wee weed in them.'

A shocked Boundy, wondering where Ronnie had left them, as he never took them off, enquired, 'Where did you leave them?'

'Aa hed them on,' was the reply.

Mr Boundy was shocked at this and scolded Ronnie with the words: 'Do you mean to tell me you stood there and let him wee wee in your wellies? Why didn't you walk away?'

Ronnie's answer 'Cos ee wasn't finished,' was the classical end to the tale, but the Bedlington Station staff never got over one of the funniest things they'd seen or heard in their teaching career.

Class 7 at Bedlington Station Primary School in 1959. Miss Marian Robinson is the teacher in charge.

Dogs Don't Like Me

Gleghorn's shop has been mentioned in passing, but it played such an important part in everyone's life in Stakeford and Bomarsund it deserves a little more comment.

Apart from being only one of two newsagents in the area at the time of my childhood, it was also the school tuck-shop and Bob & Joe Gleghorn were known by all and sundry in the area.

The shop had been the village post office, in bygone days, but Joe and Bob had it years before it was passed on to Mr Forster who didn't last long. Dave and Ann Donohoe, locals everyone knew, took on the business which Ann and son David still run.

Dave Donohoe was a character. An excellent man for the shop who always had some news about local people and incidents and a good 'crack' about Newcastle United.

One story involving Ann, Dave and myself happened in December 1978. My eldest daughter Christine informed me the *Blue Jeans* girls' magazine had a pop calendar in the new edition which had proved so popular it was sold out everywhere. 'Dad, could you get me a copy somewhere please?'

I was determined to be successful in the quest and thought of Dave straight away. His telephone response was positive but I'd have to come to the back door, through the yard, as the shop was shut.

Ten minutes later I was in Gleghorn's shop back yard where I encountered what looked like a mobile kit bag. It turned out to be the Donohoe's English bull terrier, Peter.

It growled, leered and showed an immediate dislike for me, but it didn't attack – until Ann answered the knock on the door. As soon as Ann appeared it went for me, ripped my trousers and my left leg. Ann yelled for Dave who came out armed with a poker which the dog took between its teeth and it was forced into its kennel and the door locked.

While Dave was performing this heroic act, he told me to wait outside the yard gate until he'd got the dog settled. I didn't need a second telling and limped onto the pavement.

As I waited, watching the blood ooze out of my leg onto the torn Isaac Walton best flannels, I noticed out of the corner of my eye, a tiny Yorkshire Terrier toddle up the road. It stopped, eyed me up and down, sniffed the blood, cocked its leg and peed on me.

I swear I'd never been bitten or peed on in my life, yet both incidents happened in the space of two minutes at Gleghorn's shop.

It was in a state of bewilderment that I found Dave pressing the *Blue Jeans* magazine into my hand, clapping my back and explaining, 'I think you've had enough for one night. I'll let you off with the fourteen pence for the comic.'

Dave Donohoe in his Dereham Terrace shop.

Gordon Terrace, Stakeford, from Gleghorn's Shop in 1926.

Epilogue

On reaching home and showing the family the state of my leg, I was made to go up to Bedlington Clinic to be seen by the nurse, who happened to be a parent of one of my pupils. You will imagine my embarrassment when she told me to take off my trousers and bend over so she could inject an anti-tetanus into my backside.

'Come back next week for a booster, Mr Martin,' she ordered.

Twenty-three years on and I'm still due that booster.

When Nipper Fell Out With 'Blackjack'

Jack 'Blackjack' Barber got his nickname through his love of the card game of that name. He never won and was one of those unfortunate people who are labelled 'accident prone'. Jack's friends would relate unbelievable tales of his adventures.

Jack was a champion angler, but on one unfortunate occasion he inadvertently left a box of worms in his locker at Cambois pit baths over a weekend. The heat of the place caused an unbearable stink and no-one could understand where the smell was coming from.

He was so 'untouchable' no-one would go down the pit in the cage with him. Perhaps the most fabulous story of this really loveable man was of an experience on one of his weekly trips to Newsham to see his sister.

Blackjack and his Jack Russell terrier, Nipper, were inseparable and they had reached the first set of railway gates near the top of Plessey Road. Jack was used to the gates being shut as the Newsham tankie always crossed the road at ten past eleven each morning. It had done so for the past 90 years or so and the roll on, roll off gates had dutifully opened and shut without major complications in that time. Few problems, until 'Blackjack' arrive at his usual time one Monday morning. The gates were shut as usual and our hero and his Jack Russell waited for the tankie to arrive and cross. A car drew up and another went into the back of it, resulting in two furious drivers having a go at each other. 'Blackjack' would sort the battle out and he tied the dog onto the gate while he did his peacemaking.

Unfortunately no one had told Jack and he hadn't noticed, that British Rail had erected lift up 'Continental' barriers over the weekend. Consequently Nipper was 30 feet up in the air, looking down with a combined air of disbelief and anger.

'Blackjack' soon had the dog lowered and it was perfectly OK apart from the fact that from that day on, whenever you knocked on 'Blackjack's' door, it was received with the dog's bark, only it had developed a stammer and replied with 'W..w..w..woof, w..w..woof.'

Jack Barber and friends. From left to right:
Doris Napier, Tommy Vince, Jean Barber,
Jack, Jenny Davis and Linda Nicholson.

SOME PEOPLE
AND PLACES

Tyne (Wansbeck Countess) a champion Bedlington Terrier.

Bedlington Dene titles it, but it is better known as Blyth Dene. The Furnace (Ironworks) area is the camera position showing the Free Wood walk on the right.

In later years some of the ironworks buildings became dwellings. On the right is Dene House originally built for Michael Longridge, but later housed by the Wood family of mineral water fame. The 'pop' factory was further to the right.

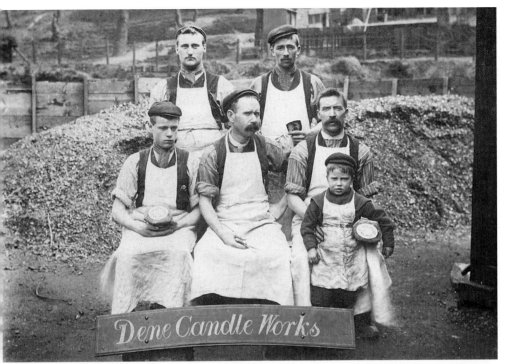

After the ironworks finally closed in 1867, some of the properties were taken over for light industries. Graham Bestford's Candle works, established in 1898, was one. Pictured here is the staff in 1908.

Inside the Candle works, the finished product on show.

Cambois folk loved their get-togethers. The Club was a popula party place. Here in the 1950s, most can be named. From the ba across: Frank Forbes, Matt Spratt Harry Riches, Eddie Matthews, Jackie Boynes, Ethel Hudspith, Gladys Spratt, Hannah Foster, Jea Hudspith. Hilda Riches, Ena Forbes, Minnie Hudspith, Meggie Payne, Janie Matthews, Charlie a Mona Smith, the two Jack Hudspiths, Gladys Thompson, Janey Armstrong, Mrs Knowles, Lizzie Henderson, Doris Pearcey, Nan Taylor, Edna Halligan, Akin Spratt, Bob Young, Jack Foster an Billy Hopper.

The figurehead of Boadicea was a landmark in Cambois for years. Situated in Hughes Bolckow's ya it was bought by Mr Mark Bamfo and shipped down to his home in Kent.

Boathouse Terrace, Cambois, looking neat and tidy.

Cambois Colliery closed in 1968 and the demolition men eventually moved in. Bridge Street doesn't look so neat and tidy.

Netherton Colliery began production in 1836 and ceased working on the 6 January 1974. Salvaging took just over three months and on the 11 April at 11.55am, E Rutter , Senior Overman and W Hamilton, Ventilation Officer, brought the last piece of coal out of the pit.

Mick Harrison in 1901. He was, at that time, the Colliery Engineer.

Monday, washing day, in First Street, Netherton.

Netherton's Wesleyan Chapel, built in 1854, was used as a garage in its last days.

The Sleekburn St John Ambulance group which won the Dr Hudson Shield in 1939. On the left standing, is Fred Hopper and seated is Tommy Corner. The Sleekburn group's headquarters was for many years opposite the Wallow (Palace) further down the road. Many miners took First Aid classes with certificates by local doctors for their feats in dealing with injuries.

West Sleekburn miners at work and play. The mechanics pose with their gear on bank in 1908.

Saturday saw some of the mechanics in the West Sleekburn side. Always known for their good competitive sides, this Winnin' team of pre-first war were Northumberland Minor Cup winners.

Bill Lockey was one of the keenest (and best) of amateur photographers up to one hundred years ago. He photographed himself Kirving in the 5/4 seam at the Old Pit in 1905. Note the candle on the pan shul (shovel).

Lockey photographed 'A' Pit fore overman Robert Wharrier and his son surveying, using a miners' dial in 1905.

One of the most important and influential men in the area for many years, was John George Weeks, who was agent – viewer for Bedlington Coal Company from 1872 to 1914.

The 1926 General Strike meant free coal was stopped as well as wages. Digging in the heap for fuel was often the order of the day across the Shire. These are 'Aad' pit families from Sleekburn.

Happier times at Sleekburn in 1912. The old recreation grounds, now the Oval Estate, were always popular. Cycle racing was one of the better liked sports and a cycle track was especially laid out down at the Stead Lane site.

The old foot bridge at East Sleekburn with the Coxon sisters taking in the view – and posing.

Not many places in Bedlingtonshire were as remote as this spot – The Whinney Hill Cottages at Simm's Wood, Stakeford. These cottages were built in 1818.

The old farmhouse, Choppington East Farm in 1906.

Guide Post cross roads circa 1935.

Hartford Bridge, Nr. Bedlington. (955)

Hartford Bridge. Always difficult to negotiate, especially by strangers, with a steep and angled approach from each side.

The Wesleyan Methodist Chapel on the Front Street at Scotland Gate. Schoolmaster, John Simpson, preached the last sermon there on a Saturday, 7th September 1974, before it was demolished. Robson's the Grocers is next door.

Barrington Colliery with Chapel Row in the foreground and Double Row behind. Numbers 1 to 9 Chapel Row were built of wood in 1842 and demolished in 1953. Numbers 10 to 21 were brick built in 1852 and pulled down in 1957. Double Row was originally named North Row, made up of 25 brick houses, built in 1875 and demolished in 1967-8.

The timber viaduct over the Willow Burn held the line to Choppington 'A' and 'B' pits. Built in 1858, it was pulled down 110 years later. The ruins of Choppington brickyard are in the background.

Doctor Pit, Bedlington, opened 1854; closed 2nd March 1968.

One of the coping stones from the top of the 'A' Pit chimney. T. Emry was one of the builders.

Demolishing the Netherton Howard Pit chimney in 1950.

Choppington 'A' Pit was closed in 1966 after working for 109 years. This is how the place looked in 1956.

Church or chapel was for many people the centre of after work or school relaxation (and not just on Sundays). None more so than the Cambois Primitive Methodist (Beach) Chapel shown here in a pen and ink sketch by Jim Branley. The chapel opened in 1869 and closed in 1978.

Relaxation of an open air kind was provided for Bedlingtonshire residents by the U.D. Council when it converted the disused filter beds at Humford Mill, between the wars. The overall cost was £250. The site is still popular in the 21st century, although the baths are long since gone. The old boiler house and pumping station are in the background of this photograph.

Bill Snowdon, winding engineman at Bomarsund Colliery. Famous for his statement at sending down the cage 'Keep ahad, we're away.'
The 'Keep ahad (ahead)' instruction dated back to the far off times when men and boys were lowered down the mine in a basket and needed to 'keep ahad' the rope in case they fell over the narrow basket edge to their death.

At the end of a day's work, Bill liked his pint at 'The Rowton', Bomarsund. He's pictured here with Ronnie Hogg, Gordon Bell, Bart Redpath and two ladies, after a day at the Miners' Picnic at Bedlington.

Cuthbert Dickinson and friend Norman. They both started work for Mr McKenzie at Cleaswell Hill Farm in 1936. Cuthbert was probably better known as a charge nurse at St Mary's Hospital, Stannington. He married Dora Dance of Stakeford. Dora was well known as the post office counter clerk at the old Stakeford Post Office in Gordon Terrace.

Bill Elliott of Melrose Terrace, Sleekburn with one of the many sets of Northumbrian pipes he made.

At Buckingham Palace in 1988 to received the MBE, is Dr John Brown (centre), his son Michael, and brother-in-law Dr Victor Purvis.

Bedlington Grammar School's Girl Guides troop *circa* 1949. Back row are Maureen Storey, Joan Nesbit, Joan Hostler. Middle row: unknown, Doris Wilkin, unknown. Front row: unknown, Brenda Johnson, unknown.

Stakeford Rowing and Swimming Club in 1912. All were miners except the Vicar of West Sleekburn, Dr Graham Good, who is fifth from the left in the back row.

Robert 'Spug' Marshall, star oarsman of Cambois Rowing Club in 1937.

Longtime Vicar of St Cuthbert's Church, Bedlington, the Rev H Osgathorp, pictured in July 1952 with Lady Ridley of Blagdon Hall. She opened the summer fete that year and is here being presented with a bouquet by Elizabeth Dinsmore of Acorn Bank Farm.

Northumberland Fusiliers Band with Jack and Andrew Dunsmore of Barrington 4th and end right of back row.

Netherton Colliery Band, 1932.

An early 1950s photograph of Cambois Colliery Band at South Park, Bedlington, for the May Day parade. Some of those pictured: Jimmy Storey, Bobby Branley, George Lavender, Clarence Milburn, Jack Dixon, Akin Spratt, Mattie Spratt, Billy Bedford, Jimmy McKenzie, George Bestford, Ernie Cowell, Joe (Bunty) Thompson, Ian Hedley, Alf Bosworth and George Lee was conductor. The tall man at the back is Jefferson Woods, nephew of film star, Stan Laurel.

Outside the Lion Garage in June 1956. There wasn't just the music competition in the band contest. There was also a prize for the smartest turnout.

Like other colliery villages, Netherton ladies had a football team in 1921, playing for money to help families during strike and lay off times.

Mrs Mary Rutter (centre) with some Choppington girls at Paisce Bush Farm. Bebside Coal Company modernised the farmhouses after the estate came into their possession in 1894. Paisce or Pace Bush was the Choppington Colliery manager's house for many years until its demolition in 1964.

Members of the Church of Christ, Bedlington Front Street, 1957.

VE Day 1945. Haig Road and Beatty Road residents gather to celebrate.

Sleekburn's Young at Heart Club in 1992. Back, left to right: Mrs Ions, Mrs Downes, Mr Adamson, Mrs Carr, Mrs Williamson, Mr Thompson. Middle row: Miss Todd, Mrs Jones, Mrs Dickinson, Mrs Fluke, Mrs Hickman, Mrs Riches. Front row: Miss Reid, Mrs Appleby, Mrs Buglass.

Netherton Women's Labour group on their annual outing.

Bedlington Women's Friendly Circle at their birthday party in 1960.

Bedlington Colliery office staff trip to Edinburgh, 1948. Those on the bus included: Jack Surtees, Ben Tait, Matt Hall, Doreen Cole, Iris Scott, John Beecroft, Mr & Mrs Bob Gordon and Mr Bruce.

Stakeford Over 60s Club committee, taken in January 1952.

Opening of the quoits bay at Bedlington Welfare Park. Councillor Dick Hindhaugh throws the first quoit, watched by Jimmy Carley (left) and others.

The 1956 Miners' Picnic and the crowd listens to every word Bessie Braddock is putting across. Bessie was probably the best known female member of the Labour Party at that time. She was a large lady in build and personality and was very popular at both the Northumberland Picnic and the Durham Gala. A Scouser, Bessie was an excellent MP who worked solidly all her life for the good of Labour-minded people.

Alf Robens MP acknowledges the crowd at the top of Bedlington Bank in 1959.

Kazoo playing jazz bands were always a feature of the Picnic. They came from all over the North East to Bedlington, hoping for a fine day, like this one in the mid 1970s.

Bill Thompson was well known for his Bedlington Cricket Club connections as well as his school teaching. This is Bill with Class 2 of Bedlington Station Primary School in 1950.

Miss Jobson's class at Bedlington Grammar School in 1949. Back row, left to right: J. Percy, B. Bates, J. Potts, J. Miley, F. Cunningham, G. Welsh, F. Martin, J. Charlton. Middle row: S. Gordon, unknown, E. Turnbull, E. Little, S. Patton, M. Jefferson, J. Stanwick, K. Wray, unknown, M. Short. Front row: B. Hostler, unknown, V. Reid, M. Clark, Miss Jobson, unknown, I. Underhill, A. Moorhead, D. Wilkin.

Margaret Clark, later Margaret Morse of West Terrace, Stakeford, watches her uncle George cobble his boots on the last, on a day in 1898. Cobbling shoes and boots was a necessary activity for families. Hammering in of Segs as kids saved a great deal of cobbler's bills. Most boys wore hobnail boots through their school days. No fancy fashions in shoes in bygone days.

A typical sitting room in the late 1920s. George McCulloch poses here in Mrs Tweedy's house in Sleekburn.

Barrington Brickworks after a boiler explosion there on 13th July 1894. Mr Weatherley, the fireman at the works, was killed. His body was found a quarter of a mile away near the railway line at Red Row.

A 1930s scene showing the Furnace Bank with Wood's 'pop' factory on the left and the Bank Top pub at the top of the picture.

Market Place in the 1930s with the Market Cross looking in need of repair. It had to wait another forty years before it was properly renovated.

A peaceful 1960s Front Street scene.

Reputedly the most popular pub in Bedlington in Victorian times. The Turk's Head, is now Somerfields supermarket.

The Neuk at the time of the First World celebrations. St Bede's School has its banner showing and the old dwellings of Rosella and Salmon Place are in the background.

Ward's shop at Bedlington Station was as popular as any for the buying of reasonably priced clothes. Here, in 1930, are staff members Renee Cramer, Nancy Tweedy, John McCarron and Johnny McGish.

The Wharton Arms as it used to be.

Many a youth was mis-spent at the roller skating, dance crazy, Clayton at Bedlington Station; here pictured in 1973.

Barrington Station brickyard in 1971 with the soon to close 'A' pit behind.

A scene wonderfully captured by local photographer, Bill Ward, of Dixon's wagon 'capsizing' in the market place in December 1968.

A drawing of The Black Bull, Front Street East in the 1920s. The Barker family were tenants there for many years.

Vulcan Place seemed a lot quieter in the 1960s than it is today.

The Lord Clyde, now The Swan, at Choppington Station in 1973 with its beautiful tiled facade standing out.

No expense spared for the suits, hats and dresses at this Edwardian Bedlington wedding.

The procession following the coffins of Sgt Barton and PC Mussell after their murders in The Sun Inn, April 1913.

Not in the Shire, but not far away, was Plessey Station, photographed here in 1911.

Howard House, Netherton Colliery. Formerly the Colliery Manager's house, now a nursing home. The original house is on the left of the picture.

St Bede's schoolboys in 1926. Some of St Bede's children travelled from various parts of Bedlingtonshire.

Barrington School's first head teacher, Ben Berkeley, enjoying the sun outside his Willowbridge house in September 1923.

The Hunter family from Cambois, *circa* 1920.

Another family from the other side of the Shire, pictured in 1903. Mr William Boll was schoolmaster in Nedderton Village for many years. His family grew up in the school house which was attached to the school in the middle of the village.

Bedlington Ladies Group at their 40th Anniversary gathering on 12th December 2000. Back row: Marjorie Stevenson, Ann Stafford, Janet Hindmarsh, Irene Adamson, Margaret Curtis, Jean Brady, Maureen Smith, Betty Snowden, Pauline Beecroft, Jennifer McClugan, Olwyn Savage, Vivian Riley, Marion Watson, Sheila Marszalkowski, Margaret Penny, Mary Allen, Rita Percy and Thelma Garbutt. Second row: Jean Epsley, Betty Robinson, Joan Smith, Veronica Davy, Hazel Cunningham, Margaret Allison, Elsie Foster, Sonia Brown, Ann Gair, Betty Grand, Elizabeth Bryant, Ethel Cochrane and Betty Edwards. Third row: Mary Young, Freda Cowell, Joan Lynn, Anne Gray, Brenda Tonge, Marquerite Hall, Ann McKay, Ginette Russell, Lilian Wilson, Nancy Nesbitt, Joan Leech, Susan Riley, Diane McDonald, Betty Holliday, Margaret Fox and Betty Greenacre. Fourth row: Isobel Garrow, Judith Martin, Marjorie Wade, Norah Robinson, Merle Rewcastle, Mark Savage (Vicar), Margaret Henderson, Pauline Giacopazzi, Ethel Elliott, Jean Carrick, Wilma Smith, Joyce Simm, Joyce Craigs and Phoebe Barr. Front row: Pam Sexton, Anne Foster, Elsie Coulson, Pat Smith, Ruth Brown, Sandra Curtis, Pam Lee, Hazel Churm and Pauline Barnes.

Getting The Wires Crossed

Brother-in-law, Ron is a generous man. He likes good food, nice wine and a new place to visit and dine anywhere in Northumberland.

When The Buccaneer first opened a number of years ago, good reports filtered through to Ron and he decided a treat was on for his wife Joan, my wife and myself.

Seeing Ron was paying I volunteered to pick up and return as my part of the night out. We arrived at the pub, had a pre-meal drink in the comfortable bar and were then shown to our table in the downstairs restaurant. The menu was quickly scanned and the waitress, Tracey, a canny lass from nearby Wembley Terrace, took the order and disappeared into the kitchen.

Tracey eventually returned with our starters, at which point Ron asked for the wine list. The young girl looked flummoxed and said, 'I'll see what I can do.'

Minutes passed, the starters were finished and Tracey re-appeared to clean up. She didn't have the wine list and informed Ron, 'It's upstairs, and quite heavy. I'll have to see the manager.'

The four of us looked at each other, puzzled as to why the manager need be involved. Five minutes later we had our answer as a plodding on the stairs made us turn our heads to witness the manager carrying a large Bush radio, carefully taking each step with caution.

'Where do you want it?' we were asked. 'There's a plug next to your table if that's OK. This is the first time since we opened I've been asked for this,' he panted.

It took us a while to realise that Tracey the waitress had mistaken Ron's request for a wine list and thought he'd said 'wireless'.

It all ended in peels of laughter. The meal was splendid and we recommended The Buccaneer to many, not just for the food and the ambience, but the extent the staff were prepared to go to, to satisfy the customer.

And There's More:

Over the last forty years some strange, invented words have been planted on my desk. Could you decipher them?

My sister got an award from the CHOOKVENBRA (Duke of Edinburgh).
My dad made me a rabbit hutch with YRNETN (wire netting).
On Saturday we played football then WADWATE (we had our tea).

And from a parent, a note:
'Sorry I can't come to Open Day. Got to see the BORIS AVAYA (Borough Surveyor).

GUESS WHERE

Ten pictures for you to identify. See if you can guess where they were taken. Answers near the back of the book:

A

B

C

D

E

F

G

H

I

J

The answers are on the next page.

A

The Masonic building at the West End which was first used for a Masonic meeting on 19th September 1899. The first Lodge in the town was St Cuthbert's Lodge which was consecrated in the Church of England School in June 1881.

B

The Old Hall and Pele tower – demolished in the late 1950s and replaced by the present Council Offices and Job Centre. The hall, with its ancient pele on the left, was originally the bailiff's residence. The bailiff was first appointed by the Bishop of Durham in 1379 and it is possible the pele, with its dungeons, was built for him, the hall coming later. The last bailiff was appointed in 1746, but the post was never taken up, as the salary was too small. In 1846 the Bishop leased the hall to James A Longridge and he used it to house workmen at his new Barrington Colliery. Bedlington Coal Company took over Barrington in 1858; the hall went with it and miners lived there until its demolition one hundred years later.

C

St Cuthbert's Church, Bedlington, *circa* 1770, from a drawing by Ralph Beilby, who was the Master of Thomas Berwick. With the growth in population in the town in early years of the nineteenth century, the church was extended in 1816 and further developed in 1911 with Squire Burdon's widow paying for the North aisle to be built. The present tower was erected in 1872.

D

The Bedlington Co-op was established in 1861 at the east end of the town, but with the expansion of the colliery village in the north west area, a large building was established, as a Co-op at the bottom of Deanery Street (now Michael Metcalf's Carpets) on Glebe Road. The success of the West End Co-op led to this building being opened on the east side of Glebe Road. Better known in later years as Bob Watson's Newsagency, it is long gone as are other buildings of the street (eg Alma Inn, Tankerville Arms, Fountain Inn Yard). The dual carriageway now occupies the area.

E

The Blue Bell Inn, Front Street, as it was in 1901. This photograph was taken from the Lion Garage side of the road. Mr Bill Forster was the publican and next door with the tiny window was Mrs Broon's Bullet Shop (sweets, not ammunition).

F

There was a toll road belonging to the Coal Company, which ran from the Lord Clyde end of Barrington Road almost to Bedlington Station. The Fletcher family ran the toll from its inception (*circa* 1869) until the road was adopted by Bedlington Coal Company in 1930. Mrs Fletcher is here performing her tollgate duties at the Choppington end of the road.

G
Netherton Village in 1903. The village of Netherton was recognised for post office purposes as Nedderton and district from the colliery at Netherton. Local farms Burnt House, Blue House and Red House have identifiable marks traced back to the early 1700s. The names were derived from the colour of the roof tiles of the early years. The landowner, Lord Carlisle, provided the local school in 1846 and it served as the village hall until very recent time. Netherton is one of the oldest mining areas in the Shire, with the nearby moor being known as 'Pitmen's Moor' from as early as the fourteenth century.

H
Stakeford to Guide Post road in 1915. Front Mowbray Terrace was newly built and the Victorian buildings on the right lasted for many years after this photograph was taken.

I
Bedlington Ironworks lasted on the Bedlington side of the River Blyth from 1736 to 1867. The chimney on the left was from the Longridge family's engineworks on the Blyth side of the water. This company produced over 400 broad and narrow gauge engines for all parts of the world from 1837 to 1855. This local newspaper photograph was taken *circa* 1902; 35 years after the works were abandoned.

J
Whitley Memorial School Camp, Rothbury, 1950. Lads enjoying their meal, are, back: Jimmy Robinson and Les Moore. Others, left to right: Jimmy Walker, Albert Haley, Brian Green, Cliff Barns, Norman Turner, Billy Moore, Tommy Reed, John Carling, George Sanderson, Cuthbert Cochrane, Joe Reed and Tom Owen. The lasses apparently were on the other side of the field.

Which leads me on to a final story, apocryphal though it is:
    After a night at a ladies 'do' in Bedlington, some years ago, a meeting entitled 'Salad Days', during which I related some of the tales foisted upon you here, I was approached by an elderly lady with a stick and a small dog. 'You're Evan Martin, Stakeford Primary School, 1946 ish!'
    'Yes I was there in those days,' I agreed.
    'I could tell a tale or two about when you were a lad.'
    My puzzled look encouraged the lady to announce she was Mary Molden and she had been my teacher in Junior School just after the war.
    I shook her hand and she sniffed and pushed her spectacles back onto the bridge of her nose (a habit she had in 1946) and I was transported back in time as she related details of a trip we'd had that year.

'Do you remember the day out we had at York racecourse just after the war? It cost 5 shillings, of which the County paid half because you'd all spent a lot of time during the war in air-raid shelters.'

I nodded but didn't speak as Mary was in full flow.

'We took Billy Appleby's bus to the Central Station, got the train to York and another bus took us on to the Knavesmire Racecourse on the Tadcaster road. When we got there you all danced, skipped, played games and sang. After all the excitement we settled down for our lunch, a Carrick's pie, Gelson's fruit bun, a bag of Hoggett's crisps and a bottle each of Muter's splits 'pop' to wash it down.

Now we hadn't been to the toilet since we got off the train and there were no conveniences there. Mrs Seeley had the idea of taking the girls to one side of the field, which she and Miss Taylor did and Mrs Green and I took you lads to the other side of the field.'

At this point I wondered what Miss Molden was getting at.

'Now there wasn't zips on your pants in those days, just buttons, which some lads were having difficulty with; so Mrs Green and I went up and down the line helping you with your unfastening and fastening. Then I came to one character, looked at him and said, Here, you're not one of our boys.'

'No,' was his reply 'I'm a jockey from the racecourse.'

Miss Molden didn't laugh out loud, but realised I'd enjoyed the story, rolled her tongue around her mouth, tapped me on the shoulder and said 'Beat that one!'

Here endeth the lesson.

Billy Appleby with one of his buses.

ALSO AVAILABLE FROM THE PEOPLE'S HISTORY

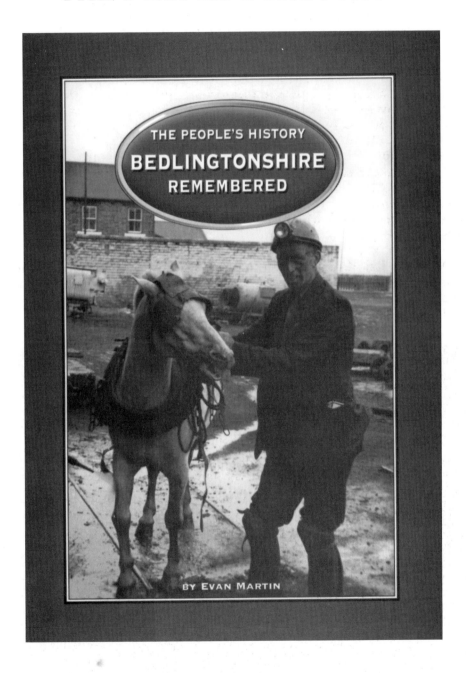

THE PEOPLE'S HISTORY

BEDLINGTONSHIRE

REMEMBERED

BY EVAN MARTIN

It is hoped you've enjoyed this book and your smile is as big as these ladies' smiles, from Cambois WI in January 1958. Pictured are, back row left to right: Ina Ferguson, Sylvia Lawson, Jean Hudspith, Eleanor Taggart, unknown, Minnie Hudspith, Mary Laverick, Amy Clark, Nancy Morrison, Marjorie Wood. Seated: Mrs Ross, Nellie Bell, Jennie Graham, Annie Dixon. Front: Mona Smith, Edna Halligon, Lizzie Taggart. On the right: Meggie Wood and Kate Bates.

The People's History

To receive a catalogue of our latest titles send a large SAE to:

The People's History
Suite 1
Byron House
Seaham Grange Business Park
Seaham
County Durham
SR7 0PY